CONSCIENCE & CONVERSION IN NEWMAN

CONSCIENCE & CONVERSION IN NEWMAN

A DEVELOPMENTAL STUDY OF SELF
IN JOHN HENRY NEWMAN

WALTER E. CONN

MARQUETTE
UNIVERSITY
PRESS

MARQUETTE STUDIES IN THEOLOGY
NO. 71
ANDREW TALLON, SERIES EDITOR

LIBRARY OF CONGRESS CATALOGING-IN-PUBLICATION DATA

Conn, Walter E.
Conscience & conversion in Newman : a developmental study of self in John Henry Newman / by Walter E. Conn.
    p. cm. — (Marquette studies in theology ; no. 71)
Includes bibliographical references and index.
ISBN-13: 978-0-87462-777-0 (pbk. : alk. paper)
ISBN-10: 0-87462-777-X (pbk. : alk. paper)
1. Newman, John Henry, 1801-1890. 2. Conversion—Catholic Church. 3. Catholic converts—England. 4. Conscience. 5. Self. I. Title.
BX4705.N5C66 2010
282.092—dc22

2010000476

Marquette University Press
Milwaukee, Wisconsin 53201-3141
All rights reserved.
www.marquette.edu/mupress/

FOUNDED 1916

COVER DESIGN AND ART BY COCO CONNOLLY

♾ The paper used in this publication meets the minimum requirements of the
American National Standard for Information Sciences—
Permanence of Paper for Printed Library Materials, ANSI Z39.48-1992.

Association of American
University Presses

MARQUETTE UNIVERSITY PRESS
MILWAUKEE

The Association of Jesuit University Presses

CONTENTS

Preface 7

1. Young Man Newman: The First Conversion 13

2. Newman's Cognitive Conversion to Anglo-Catholicism 26

3. From Oxford Tractarian to Roman Convert 51

4. The Roman Catholic Newman and Conscience 96

Epilogue 123

Appendix 125

Notes 134

Index 152

TO JOANN

PREFACE

I am the proud owner of a black Jack Daniel's T-shirt. On the upper left front is Jack's name in small white letters. On the back is a large colorful portrait of Jack sporting a full black beard and a wide-brimmed white hat. Below the picture is the motto: "Not subject to Change. Not Now. Not Ever." Now this may be a great philosophy for Tennessee sour mash whiskey, but as a philosophy of life, I submit, it misses the target by a wide margin.[1] Indeed, one of John Henry Newman's most famous quotations states exactly the opposite: "To live is to change, and to be perfect is to have changed often."[2] Newman (1801-90) wrote this just as he was about to make—at almost exactly mid-life—one of the most important, and certainly best known, changes in his own life: his 1845 conversion from the Anglican Church to the Roman Catholic Church.

A conversion is a kind of positive change, a type of development, more or less radical, that shifts the direction of one's life. Certainly Newman's conversion from the Church of England to Roman Catholicism changed the direction of his life in many important ways, but it was neither his first nor even his most personally profound conversion. While acknowledging the enormous impact of this conversion of 1845, in this study I place it in the context of a series of conversions Newman experienced.

Conversion patterns vary significantly in different persons. In an earlier study, I uncovered in Thomas Merton the four fundamental conversions outlined in the present book's Appendix (first, basic Christian moral conversion, coupled with Merton's move to Roman Catholicism; then, affective, critical moral, and religious conversions, in that order).[3] Examining Newman's life, I found that he also began with a basic Christian moral conversion (at a slightly earlier age than Merton), but that things then unfolded quite differently, with his move from the Anglican to the Roman Church, for example, coming only many years later. Here, in successive chapters, I consider Newman's series of conversions in chronological order.

First, in chapter 1, I focus on the conversion (1816) Newman experienced about three decades before his move to Rome, when the young man who would become one of the most famous men in England and the entire Catholic world—as Anglican cleric, leader of the Oxford Tractarians, controversial convert to Roman Catholicism, founder of the Catholic University of Ireland, and finally cardinal—was only fifteen. Through this conversion he moved from the conventional values of the Anglican Christianity inherited from his parents to a deeply personal Evangelical faith. In conversation with major developmental psychologists, I consider this youthful experience as a prime example of basic Christian moral conversion, with important affective, cognitive, and religious dimensions.[4] Such a conversion determines the shape of one's moral universe: it creates the core of one's character, and establishes the horizon of meaning and value for one's every discovery, decision, and deed. Nothing is more central, more fundamental, more vital to the Christian moral life.[5]

Then, in chapter 2, I examine another conversion Newman experienced in his later twenties, a structural cognitive conversion which effected a shift from his Evangelical faith to an Anglo-Catholic form of Christianity. This new faith stance formed the personal basis for the next major phase of his life—the political Tractarian Movement that sought to transform the Church of England.

In chapter 3, I analyze the complexities of Newman's famous move from Oxford to Rome, his ecclesial conversion from the Anglican Church to the Roman Church. Here I suggest a new interpretation of this move in terms of a distinction between negative deconversion and positive conversion, and a delineation of three two-year phases specified respectively by intellectual analysis and judgment, discernment and judgment of conscience, and deliberation and decision.

The legacy of John Henry Newman is as complex as he was. Some extreme authors have demonized him; others would canonize him. A *via media*, with warts as well as dimples, may offer a more realistic portrait.[6] I make significant use of Newman's autobiographical writings, especially his *Apologia pro Vita Sua*, but critically complement these with his voluminous *Letters and Diaries* and other sources.[7] During and since the Second Vatican Council both liberal and conservative Catholics have claimed him as their own. But his life and work resist any easy labeling. This study reveals within Newman's many facets a singleness of self, a self driven through his series of far reaching conversions by the creative force of a unifying, dynamic conscience. In chapter 4, finally, I examine three key dimensions of Newman's understanding of conscience, and propose an integrating interpretation in terms of a radical desire for a transcendent Other, the ultimate reality of truth, goodness, and love.

This volume is not primarily a biography of Newman; there are already many fine biographies on which I have relied, especially those by Ian Ker and Sheridan Gillley, as will be evident throughout.[8] I do hope, however, that some readers will find in it a useful review of Newman's life. Nor is this a detailed study of Newman's writings; excellent ones abound, and I have benefited from them. This rather is a study *in* Newman, a study of conscience and conversion as these profound realities formed and transformed the life and thought of one of the English-speaking world's great Christian leaders and thinkers.

Books rarely turn out to be all their authors had hoped them to be. This one is no exception. A major regret for me is my lack of courage in abandoning the idea I originally had for its title: Newman's Own Development. Also, I almost regret not having another ten years for this book; instead, I have a book, imperfect as it is.

The virtues of solitude notwithstanding, one rarely writes a book alone. I am grateful for the editorial advice of Lawrence Cunningham and Edward Miller who read earlier versions of this work; for the support of colleagues and administrators at Villanova University; for the cooperation of editors at Paulist Press, Marquette University Press, *Theological Studies*, and the *Journal of Newman Studies*, who first published sections (Preface, chap. 1 and Appendix; chap. 2; chap. 3; and chaps. 3 and 4, respectively) of this work in earlier versions and allowed their inclusion here; and especially for the patient and comprehensive editorial advice of Andrew Tallon at Marquette University Press.

I dedicate this book with love to sweet Joann, my Cozy Home Companion and Resident Artist, and recognize our dear friends who have supported me through many years of research and writing, especially Eileen Flanagan and Therese Bell of Willistown Chase, Mary Ann Hinsdale of Somerville, Jane and Chuck Hanson of Brewster on the Bay (with their Mossdoos), Judy and Rodger Van Allen of Woodstock Farm, Geraldine A. Bloemker, M.A. (*Villa.*) and Michael Garrity of Havertown on the Main Line, Angela Keane of Clondalkin, Jo Anne and Don McGuigan of Paoli Woods, Charlie Curran of the Diocese of Rochester, my rare lunch companion and Christmas train dispatcher Sue Toton and Jerry Zurek of Valley Forge, and Mary Jo and Joe Walheim and our other wonderful friends in Eagles Mere. They are blessings all.

In previous books I have acknowledged my profound debt to Bernard J. F. Lonergan (1904-84) and Joseph F. X. Flanagan, both of the Society of Jesus; I gratefully do so again. And here, appropriately for a study in Newman, I honor in memory a third Jesuit, recently deceased at ninety, Avery Dulles, a gentleman, scholar, convert to Rome, priest, and, also like Newman, in later years a member of the College of Cardinals.

I treasure the fellowship of our Sunday morning Holy Donut group (Maria Sowerby, founder) as well as the entire liturgical community at the Medical Mission Sisters in Fox Chase. I delight in the camaraderie of our tennis groups in Bryn Mawr and Eagles Mere.

I give special thanks for decades of loving care to my inspiring sister Fran and brother-in-law Charlie Gilchrist of North Grafton. One other person who has known and loved me as long as Fran is my cousin Tom Millerick of Green Hill (I still remember the baseball spikes he gave to a fledgling ballplayer, the Little Man, for his first game more than sixty years ago); he and his lovely Eileen have my warmest gratitude. This book is offered in loving memory of Tom's sister, Elizabeth Millerick Bryan, my dear cousin.

—The Long Retreat, Eagles Mere, August 11, 2009

I like middles. It is in middles that extremes clash,
where ambiguity restlessly
rules.

—John Updike

I. YOUNG MAN NEWMAN
THE FIRST CONVERSION

I. CHILDHOOD AND EARLY ADOLESCENCE

John Henry Newman was born in London on February 21, 1801. He was the first of John and Jemima (*née* Fourdrinier) Newman's six children, followed quickly by Charles, Harriett, Francis, Jemima, and, in 1809, Mary. His parents were conventional Christians of the established Church of England, and John Henry was baptized on April 9, 1801 in the Church of St. Benet Fink. Decades later, in his *Apologia pro Vita Sua* (1864), Newman wrote of his early religious life: "I was brought up from a child to take great delight in reading the Bible; but I had no formed religious convictions till I was fifteen. Of course I had a perfect knowledge of my Catechism."[1] John Henry's paternal grandmother and Aunt Elizabeth were largely responsible for his religious education.

With the father in banking, the Newmans were what today we would call an upper middle-class family. In addition to a five-storied Georgian town house in Bloomsbury, there was a large country house in Ham, Grey Court House. One of Newman's earliest memories was lying in bed at Grey Court watching the window candles flame in celebration of Nelson's 1805 victory at Trafalgar. More than fifty years later he recalled this and another memory of Grey Court in a letter to his sister Jemima: "I have lately been to see our house at Ham, which we had before you were born,—where I was when you were born; and whence I sent my Mother by my Father the present of a broom-flower on your birth." Although the family had Grey Court for only a few years, it had a profound impact on John Henry's imagination and always remained vivid in his memory. In 1832, while on a Mediterranean trip, Newman wrote, in a Platonic, Romantic key, of how he "thought of Ham and of all the various glimpses ... of that earliest time of life when one seems almost to realize the remnant of a pre-existent state."[2]

Letters and diaries tell us of a happy family life filled with music, dancing, reading, and theater-going. Here were nurtured the beginnings of John Henry's expertise on the violin and his life-long love of literature. Most importantly, this bright and affectionate family was the perfect nursery for the very young John Henry's cognitive and affective life. Family enthusiasm for learning is reflected clearly in a letter Mr. Newman wrote to his oldest son when John Henry was only five, but could already read perfectly. "My dear John Henry, This is the first Letter your Papa ever wrote to his Son. I request you will read it to your Mamma and also to Charles that, when he sees how well you can read writing, he will be very desirous of minding his Book that he may also be able to do the same—but you will observe that you must learn something new every Day, or you will no longer be called a clever Boy." As he continues, John Henry's father is not above a bit of academic bribery: "I therefore hope that by Thursday next you will have got your Multiplication Table by Heart and have also began to learn your Pence Table. I mean to examine you as to your Multiplication Table and if I find you improve I intend after a time to buy you a nice Copy Book and teach you to write."[3]

As the oldest, John Henry was the leader among the siblings, and he became the responsible one, but his brothers especially were never docile enough to allow him to become overbearing. The warm and lively relationships among parents and children brought out the best in John Henry's sensitive nature, and many mutual relationships of loving care are manifest in countless letters over the years.

When he was only seven John Henry was sent off to a private boarding school at Ealing. A bit younger and more sensitive than most of the other boys, he endured some bullying for a while. But his natural abilities soon blossomed, and before long he was not only excelling in his studies, but editing school periodicals and even founding and leading a secret group of students—The Spy Club. Neither his abilities nor his interest seem to have extended to athletic games, though like most boys of his time he rode horseback, and did a lot of hiking and boating. His great interests were mainly literary—writing for the school papers, reciting in Greek, acting in Latin plays. In free moments he especially delighted in the Romantic adventures of Walter Scott's new novels. The headmaster, the Rev. Dr. George Nicholas, thought John Henry was one of the best students ever at Ealing. And John Henry's high regard for Ealing and its headmaster became clear when he argued successfully against his father's plan to have him transfer to Winchester. In general, Ealing helped develop the strong imagination John Henry had brought to school, while inspiring and training his considerable intellectual powers. During these school years he also learned to control a very strong will and temper, though he remained somewhat shy and introverted.[4] The younger brothers Charles and Francis followed John Henry to Ealing, and close contact was maintained with his sisters through many wonderfully affectionate letters. One example, to Jemima, reveals John Henry's distinctive sense of humor: he begins, "It is always a great pleasure to me to write to you, for the following reason. If I write to Harriett she always requires a laughable letter, which is by no means suited to the dignity of my character, but you Jemima being conspicuously and wonderfully sedate yourself, always like a serious, sedate, sensible epistle." Then he gets to his main joke: "One thing in your letter disappointed me very much, and this it was. At the end you say, we all send our love with your affectionate sister, J. C. Newman. I consequently very naturally supposed that you were sent to me, as your letter seemed to imply it, and as there was a lumbering *heavy* lump of something or other at the bottom of the parcel, I concluded it must be you, and so I began to unpack this rapidly, to give you (as I thought) some fresh air, of which I did not doubt that you were in want. When to my surprise, having unpacked the said heavy lump, it proved to be a cake!"[5]

As he celebrated his fifteenth birthday, John Henry's family life and school life were all he could have hoped for.

2. A DEVELOPMENTAL PERSPECTIVE

From a developmental perspective John Henry by this point seems to have successfully negotiated the first four of psychoanalyst Erik Erikson's eight affective life-cycle tasks. *Trust*, the psychosocial bedrock of religious faith, was established early on in infancy through healthy parental relationships, and was later strengthened by a caring headmaster at Ealing, not damaged as often happened at English public schools of the time. Everything we know about John Henry indicates that the issue of *autonomy* was handled well at the toddler stage. Throughout childhood he had, as we say, a will of his own. He managed to get his way, as we noted, about the proposed transfer to Winchester, and he displayed a strong will even when he failed to get what he wanted. On one occasion when his mother emphasized his failure to prevail, he responded, "No, but I tried very hard."[6] For Erikson, *initiative* is the ability to act deliberately with purpose, unimpeded by excessive guilt. The superego, what Erikson calls the "great governor of initiative," emerges in the pre-school years and creates a radical division and estrangement within the self. Though a narrowly moralistic internalization of parental control, this inner voice of self-observation, self-regulation, and self-punishment is a necessary foundation for the adult's mature ethical conscience. The leadership John Henry exercised first among his siblings and later at school clearly reflects a healthy ratio of initiative over guilt in these early years, which in turn established a lively but moderate superego foundation for the conscience that would become Newman's hallmark. The early school period is the crisis time of *industry* versus inferiority, when a foundation must be laid for a future sense of competence. For John Henry this meant academic achievement, and we have already seen how he excelled in his studies from the very beginning—even before he went off to Ealing. This early academic accomplishment helped to create the boy and young man who as an adult would become one of the great scholars of his time.

This academic competence was rooted, of course, in young John Henry's developing cognitive abilities. Jean Piaget, the Swiss developmental psychologist, has delineated four key stages of cognitive development: sensorimotor, preoperational, concrete operational, and formal operational. By the end of his fifteenth year John Henry's academic prowess clearly demonstrated his possession of the complex, abstract thinking of fully formal operations. In addition, his accomplished violin skills indicate an advanced training of sensitive sensorimotor abilities, and his poetic imagination displays a highly sophisticated degree of preoperational thinking's symbolic powers. Young John Henry was not only intellectually brilliant, but his brilliance was well rounded and balanced; cognitively, he appears to have had it all.

In this affective and cognitive basis John Henry's moral and faith development were well rooted. By early adolescence he appears to have broached the third stages of both moral and faith development as delineated by contemporary American researchers Lawrence Kohlberg and James Fowler respectively. In terms of moral reasoning, though not yet consistent action, John Henry seems comfortably set in a conventional orientation in which it is important not only to conform to but also maintain, support, and justify the social order and its values, rules, and expectations. At moral stage three (*Interpersonal Concordance*), this conventional orientation focuses on caring for others and being a good person, in one's own eyes as well as others'. Individual interests are no longer primary, as in earlier stages.

For James Fowler, faith (or, more accurately, active "faithing") is a knowing, a construing, or an interpreting of experience in light of a person's relatedness to those "sources of power and values which impinge on life in a manner not subject to personal control." Faithing involves the whole person—cognitive, affective, moral. Following the Intuitive-Projective and Mythic-Literal stages of childhood, Fowler delineates a third, *Synthetic-Conventional* stage that can appear as early as adolescence but often later, and may endure through an adult's entire life. As formal cognitive operations emerge, and as a person's world extends beyond family and primary social groups, faithing "must help provide a coherent and meaningful synthesis of that now more complex and diverse range of involvements."[7] At this stage a person's world of meaning is mediated by symbols dwelt in precritically, that is, as unexamined, taken for granted givens (e.g., a particular image or concept of God). Though often expressed in theological language, faithing is a universal human reality, and not necessarily "religious" in the ordinary sense of the word. Indeed, John Henry, at age fourteen, having been influenced by writers like Thomas Paine and Voltaire and possibly David Hume, desired to be virtuous, but not religious. "There was something in the latter idea I did not like. Nor did I see the *meaning* of loving God," he later wrote. He agreed with Alexander Pope's *Essay on Man*: "Virtue alone is happiness below."[8]

These affective, cognitive, moral, and faith elements are all dimensions of the whole *self*. The contemporary American psychologist Robert Kegan has focused explicitly on the structural development of the self—development, that is, not in terms of some particular content (e.g., sexual), but in terms of making the self's meaning through successively different ways of relating (separating/attaching) to others. In Kegan's schema John Henry at his fifteenth birthday was likely verging on the third stage of the *Interpersonal* self, which follows upon the Impulsive and Imperial selves of childhood. The Interpersonal self has emerged from being embedded in its own self-interest needs, and thus is no longer subject to them. This self can coordinate its needs with those of others, becoming "mutual, empathic, and oriented to reciprocal obligation."[9] But it now *is* that shared reality; unable to reflect on the expectations, satisfactions, and obligations of that shared reality, it is now subject to it. Conflict at this stage is not principally between the self and others, but within a self that is part of various shared realities. Adolescents, for example, can feel torn apart by opposing loyalties to parents, teachers, and other authority figures on the one hand, and to members of their peer group on the other. So, developmentally, John Henry's willfully trusting and purposefully competent self, with its formal operations and budding stagethree structural components, is essentially what would be expected of an extremely bright adolescent with a sense of values, warm family relationships, and confident leadership qualities. Life was good, and John Henry was happy. But then everything suddenly changed.

3. JOHN HENRY'S CONVERSION EXPERIENCE

On March 8, 1816, John Henry's father's bank closed its doors for the last time, one of the many victims of an economic crisis that followed upon the end of the Napoleonic wars. All the depositors were finally paid, so John Henry never referred to it as a failure. But his father, nearly fifty, was faced with very difficult financial circumstances, and the family thus experienced something of a crisis of its own. Before too long, however, Mr. Newman, with the help of his partners, was able to secure a position managing a brewery in Hampshire, and he and Mrs. Newman moved the household there, to Jane Austen's Alton. The boys were at school, and the girls stayed with their grandmother and Aunt Elizabeth while their parents planned and executed the move. As the oldest of the children, and already a confidant of his parents, John Henry had been called home from school for a few days to be briefed on the traumatic situation. With his keen sense of responsibility he surely shared deeply in the sense of vulnerability his parents were experiencing as their former prosperous life fell to pieces. He returned to school and remained there during the summer and fall, beyond the completion of his studies. A letter of the time from Mrs. Newman to her sister-in-law Elizabeth conveys something of his parents' concerns. While keeping herself "prepared for the worst," John Henry's mother shares with Elizabeth her "ardent wish" that the bank affairs be handled quietly, "so as no one may be injured, and we retain our name unsullied … ." Then her personal optimism comes through as she focuses on the silver lining: "my kind love to your Mother, I hope she will not distress herself about us. Tell her I feel confident the trial although severe will prove for our permanent good and increase our happiness. John and I already love each other with increased affection. We begin to see the bottom of each other's heart, he begs me to say everything kind and affecte [sic] to you both." And she ends in gratitude: "What shall I say to you in thanks for your kindness and comfort you yield me, in protecting my dear Children and persevering in their education in my absence with my dear John, whom of course I shall not leave while things are any ways unsettled, indeed I assure you it relieved me from a weight that would be too heavy for me to bear, if they were not continued in a proper train and had cause to lament our absence."[10]

In early August, while the other students were on summer vacation, John Henry became seriously ill. Though his life was not threatened, he long remembered this feverish sickness as one of his "three great illnesses." Many years later he wrote of it as the "first keen, terrible one, when I was a boy of 15, and it made me a Christian—with experiences before and after, awful, and known only to God." He recollected how, while still reeling from the bank closing and now racked by fever, he was "terrified at the heavy hand of God which came down upon me."[11] Lonely, feverish, uncertain about his future, John Henry's once happy, active, secure life was suddenly shattered. Virtue alone, perhaps, was not enough.

It was in this dazed, confused, weak state of vulnerability that John Henry experienced his first conversion. Converted individuals often exaggerate the difference between their before and after conversion selves, emphasizing the evil of their pre-conversion self in a way that others might not recognize. Whether John Henry exaggerated or not, he did emphasize his pre-conversion evil when he later recollected the conversion experience. Addressing God in a journal entry more than four decades later, the mature Newman wrote: "Thy wonderful grace turned me right round when I was more like a devil than a wicked boy ... ."[12] He asked, "Was any boyhood so impious as some years of mine? Did I not in fact dare Thee to do Thy worst?"[13] Newman was likely referring to the skepticism we have already noted in the adolescent influenced by Paine, Hume, and Voltaire, seeing in it a diabolical intellectual pride, self-will, and self-sufficiency. In 1844 he had written to his friend John Keble along the same lines: "When I was a boy of fifteen and living a life of sin, with a very dark conscience and a very profane spirit, He mercifully touched my heart." Near the end of his life, in order to emphasize the radicality of this experience, the octogenarian Cardinal Newman wrote: "It is difficult to realize or imagine the identity of the boy before and after August 1816 .... I can look back at the end of seventy years as if on another person."[14]

In his 1864 *Apologia*, which he cast as a history of his "Religious Opinions," Newman described this intense conversion experience as "a great change of thought," emphasizing the intellectual dimension of this deeply personal transformation.[15] Focusing on the theological articulation of his experience, he wrote of falling under "the influences of a definite Creed" and receiving into his "intellect impressions of dogma, which, through God's mercy, have never been effaced or obscured." At the time of his conversion, Evangelicalism had become a major force, both inside the established Church of England and outside of it among Methodists and other Dissenters. Newman credited one of his classics teachers, the Rev. Walter Mayers, a relatively recent Evangelical convert himself, as being "the human means of this beginning of divine faith" in him. Mayers influenced John Henry at this impressionable time through conversations and sermons, but especially through the books he recommended, all of a Calvinist perspective. One of the first of these influential books John Henry read was a work by William Romaine, an eighteenth-century English Evangelical divine. By the time he wrote his *Apologia* Newman had forgotten the book's title and most of its contents, but he clearly remembered its doctrine of final perseverance, even though he no longer believed it to be a doctrine of divine origin. He wrote: "I received it at once, and believed that the inward conversion of which I was conscious, (and of which I still am more certain than that I have hands and feet,) would last into the next life, and that I was elected to eternal glory" (he never accepted predestination of the damned, however). At the time of the *Apologia* Newman recalled that this conviction of perseverance, which lasted some half dozen years, had directed his mind along the lines of his childhood fantasies: "in isolating me from the objects which surrounded me, in confirming me in my mistrust of the reality of material phenomena, and making me rest in the thought of two and two only absolute and luminously self-evident beings, myself and my Creator ... ."[16] A few years after the experience, the young Newman had written: "The reality of conversion:—as cutting at the root of doubt, providing a chain between God and the soul. (i.e. with every link complete) I know I am right. How do you know it? I know I know. How? I know I know I know &c &c."[17]

Perhaps the most important influence of all following his conversion experience was the writing of Thomas Scott. In his *Apologia* Newman remembered Scott as "the writer who made a deeper impression on my mind than any other, and to whom (humanly speaking) I almost owe my soul ... ." He had been impressed by Scott's "bold unworldliness and vigorous independence of mind." It is not surprising that John Henry, in his idealistic dedication to intellectual rigor, would be inspired by Scott, who "followed truth wherever it led him, beginning with Unitarianism, and ending in a zealous faith in the Holy Trinity." About the Trinity, the mature Newman wrote that it was Scott "who first planted deep in my mind that fundamental truth of religion." Newman also admired Scott's practicality, and recalled in the *Apologia* two characteristic thoughts of Scott's teaching which also tellingly reflect Newman's own life and teaching: "*Holiness rather than peace,*" and "*Growth the only evidence of life.*"

Newman recounts in the *Apologia* how at this critical time he was deeply influenced by the works of two other authors: "each contrary to each, and planting in me the seeds of an intellectual inconsistency which disabled me for a long course of years." He explains how his reading of Bishop Thomas Newton's *Dissertations on the Prophecies* convinced him that the pope was the Antichrist predicted by Daniel, St. Paul, and St. John. So profound was Newton's influence that the "false conscience" it created in the young Newman's imagination lasted over a quarter of a century, until 1843, long after it had been erased from his reason and judgment. At the same time as he was reading Newton, John Henry was also working through Joseph Milner's volumes on the *History of the Church of Christ*, and was "nothing short of enamoured" of its long extracts from St. Augustine, St. Ambrose, and other writers of the early church. These great early Christian authors offered him a union of reason and symbol that would finally aid him, after "many years of intellectual unrest," in integrating his own extraordinary powers of intellect and imagination. But that would take much further study, prayer, and time.

John Henry's conversion experience caused him to feel the need for some behavioral changes—a stricter life, penance. But most of all, as Newman reluctantly recounts in the *Apologia*, a "deep imagination ... took possession" of him: "that it would be the will of God that I should lead a single life." This anticipation of celibacy was connected in his mind with the sense of a calling to a life of sacrifice, possibly "missionary

work among the heathen." Newman concludes the *Apologia's* attention to his youthful conversion experience by remarking that this "deep
imagination" about the single life strengthened his "feeling of separation from the visible world."

A year after his conversion the young Newman reflected the personal depth and moral character of the experience in a prayer of thanksgiving: "for thy goodness in enlightening my soul with the knowledge of thy Truth; that whereas I was proud, self-righteous, impure,
abominable and altogether corrupt in my sinful imaginations, thou
wast pleased to turn me to thee from such a state of darkness and irreligion by a mercy which is too wonderful for me; and to make me fall
down humbled and abased before thy foot-stool."[18] Still, despite the
thoroughgoingness of the experience, and despite the guidance of the
Evangelical Rev. Mayers, before too many years the young Newman
became aware that "he had not been converted in that special way
which [Evangelicals] laid down as imperative, but so plainly against
rule, as to make it very doubtful in the eyes of normal evangelicals
whether he had really been converted at all." He had not experienced
the sudden and violent Evangelical "stages of conviction of sin, terror,
despair, news of the free and full salvation, apprehension of Christ,
sense of pardon, assurance of salvation, joy and peace, and so on to
final perseverance."[19] And he was wary of excessive enthusiasm. His
experience, as he later described it, was more like "a returning to, a
renewing of, principles, under the power of the Holy Spirit, which I
had already felt, and in a measure acted on, when young." And he had a
strong moral sense of the need to continue growing in holiness. At the
same time, he realized that his entire being was different: "I know and
am sure that before I was blind, but now I see." Although the radical
personal conversion he experienced was real and undeniable, his initial
theological articulation of it in Evangelical terms was not a good fit.
But if John Henry did not undergo an Evangelical conversion, exactly
how shall we understand his profound experience?

4. UNDERSTANDING JOHN HENRY'S
CONVERSION

Conversion changes the direction of one's life. It is an "about-face"
which moves one into a new world, creates a radically new horizon. More than an expansion of previous horizontal development,

conversion, Bernard Lonergan asserts, is a vertical move which "begins a new sequence that can keep revealing ever greater depth and breadth and wealth." It "affects all of a man's conscious and intentional operations. It directs his gaze, pervades his imagination, releases the symbols that penetrate to the depths of his psyche. It enriches his understanding, guides his judgments, reinforces his decisions."[20] The second set of four crises or tasks of Erikson's life cycle offers a developmental context for distinguishing four basic types of conversion. Although my central point is that John Henry's conversion—despite obvious affective, cognitive, and religious qualities—was primarily a basic Christian moral conversion, it is important to recognize other conversion possibilities in order to appreciate the serious limits as well as the significant achievement of this profound experience.

First, Erikson's interpretation of the *identity* crisis in terms of a commitment of fidelity to value distinguishes an intrinsically moral dimension in adolescent conversion. From Kohlberg's perspective on moral development, basic *moral conversion* corresponds to the transition from preconventional to conventional moral reasoning. Fundamentally, this transition is a shift from an egocentric orientation in which the criterion for decision is self-interested satisfaction to a social orientation in which the criterion is value.

Next, the young adult's Eriksonian crisis of *intimacy*, with its defining strength of love, may be the occasion of an *affective conversion*. If moral conversion challenges us to move beyond ourselves, we meet that challenge only when we fall in love, only when we escape the centripetal force of our egocentric gravity. Kegan's analysis of how at his fifth stage an Interindividual self emerges that is capable of sharing itself, while remaining distinct, offers a structural interpretation of affective conversion rooted in the distinction between pre-identity fusion and post-identity intimacy.

Further, the *generativity* of Erikson's adult ethical orientation, characterized by care and responsibility, suggests a moral conversion beyond conventional values. Indeed, Kohlberg's postconventional level of moral reasoning, rooted in self-chosen, universal ethical principles, requires not only this strength of generativity, but also a cognitive conversion—the critical discovery of the criterion of the real and valuable not somewhere "out there" but in one's own realistic judgment. From Piaget's perspective, such a conversion is rooted in the adult's integration of adolescent formal reasoning with the empirical dimension of concrete operations into the power of realistic judgment. Thus *critical moral conversion* goes beyond conventional values by grounding value in the reality of oneself as a critical, originating value.

Finally, Fowler's distinction between Stage 3 Synthetic-Conventional Faith and Stage 4 Individuative-Reflexive Faith presupposes the same cognitive conversion to a critical standpoint of being one's own authority. Indeed, Fowler's analysis extends to a postcritical Stage 6 Universalizing Faith, whose sense of ultimate environment includes all being. This radical structural de-centering is correlative to Erikson's final life-cycle task of *integrating* life's meaning. This is what theologians mean by a *religious conversion*, which radically reorients one's entire life by allowing God to move from the periphery to the center of one's being—a total falling-in-love with a mysterious, uncomprehended God. Such religious conversion is "total and permanent self-surrender without conditions, qualifications, reservations."[21]

Such are the fundamental conversion possibilities: basic moral, affective, (cognitive) critical moral, and religious. Throughout his life Newman, with greater responsibilities, deeper affective experiences, and more advanced cognitive self-possession, may have experienced all four conversions. Whatever may be true about his later life, however, the point I am making here is that John Henry's profound experience at age fifteen was a basic moral conversion rooted in Christian values. As a fully personal experience it had, of course, important affective, cognitive, and religious qualities, but it was fundamentally a shift to value—the God of Jesus Christ—as criterion for decision. The immature conscience that had budded when John Henry was a young boy was now blossoming into the consolidated achievement of an established Christian conscience (though perhaps with a moralism that called for greater affective development).

Ever since William James' *Varieties of Religious Experience* (1902), written about a decade after Newman's death, adolescence has been seen as a privileged time for conversion. While James regarded adolescent conversions as religious experiences, Erikson, a half century later, provided a new theoretical context for understanding them in terms of the typically adolescent crisis of identity. Here the adolescent is searching for value, embodied in a person or ideology, in which he or she can, in fidelity, invest the self's life. The appropriate response to this search is moral conversion, which may or may not be more or less explicitly religious in imagery, language, and coloration, but will often be highly emotional. If the shift in criterion to the discovered value represents the object-pole of moral conversion, it is rooted at the subject-pole in the existential moment when we discover for ourselves "that it is up to each of us to decide for himself what he is to make of himself."[22] This discovery of the moral self is a common feature of the late adolescent blossoming of identity, but it is limited by the socially defined nature of identity at this period. Thus the typical adolescent conversion is a basic moral conversion to value understood conventionally, not the critical, postconventional moral conversion that requires cognitive self-possession and specifically adult experiences. Even less is conversion in adolescence the mature falling-in-love that is affective conversion or, in its unconditional form, religious conversion, both of which presuppose the identity resolution of moral conversion as a condition, that is, require the possession of a self to surrender.

The conversion experience of the fifteen-year-old John Henry—of being saved from sin by a gracious God—fits perfectly into this pattern of basic moral conversion. The maturing Newman would refine and re-define this deeply transforming experience at various points throughout his life. Fidelity to conscience leads to ever more profound conversion. But that is another story—or, actually, other stories, for other chapters. This story has been about John Henry's first conversion—the radical experience in which he discovered both himself and his God, and thus determined the course of the rest of his life. Quite simply, in his sixteenth year John Henry became a new man.

2. NEWMAN'S COGNITIVE CONVERSION
TO ANGLO-CATHOLICISM

In 1816, as we have just seen in chapter 1, John Henry Newman experienced the most important event of his life—a profound personal conversion at age fifteen, moving him from the conventional Anglican Christianity inherited from his parents to a deeply meaningful Evangelical faith. There I argued that this first conversion of 1816 is best understood as a basic Christian moral conversion, with significant cognitive, affective, and religious dimensions. Three decades later, as we will see in chapter 3, Newman, in the most famous event of his life, would convert from the Church of England to the Church of Rome in 1845. Here, in this second chapter, I will explain how these two conversions are linked by another conversion, a cognitive conversion which effected Newman's shift from an Evangelical to an Anglo-Catholic form of Christianity. I will trace the many influences on, and phases of, this cognitive conversion and religious shift through the 1820s, the third decade of Newman's life. Specifically, we will follow Newman as he moved from Evangelical, through Liberal, to High Church theology. In this development we will see a critical stage of Newman's lifelong search for truth in his fidelity to conscience, the radical drive for self-transcendence.

Cognitive conversion is a complex, multifaceted reality. We can specify it by making a basic distinction in knowing between content and structure. Content conversion in knowing is simply a significant change in *what* one knows, a change in one's views or beliefs, be they aesthetic, political, religious, or whatever. For example, before he discovered the true meaning of Christmas, Linus Van Pelt (Beethoven aficionado of "Peanuts" fame) believed in Santa Claus; but no longer. Now, with the wisdom of age, he believes in the Great Pumpkin. In contrast, structural conversion is a transformation in *how* one knows. For example, Jean Piaget distinguishes between the concrete thinking typical of childhood and the abstract thinking first available in adolescence. Or we may consider how the responsibilities of adult experience make possible a shift from uncritical to critical thinking, from being dependent on authoritative others in one's knowing to standing independently on one's own cognitive feet. Fundamentally, cognitive conversion is a new, more accurate understanding of the nature of one's knowing, most radically in the realization that the criterion of truth is not external but within one's own drive for self-transcendence.[1] In the following pages we will note signs of these various aspects of cognitive conversion (content and structure) as Newman advances from adolescence into early adulthood.

I. HEADING OFF TO OXFORD

John Henry's five-month process of conversion to Evangelicalism at age fifteen was nearing its end when, on December 14, 1816, he went off to Oxford with his father and the Rev. John Mullens, a family friend and curate of St. James, Piccadilly. Mr. Mullens, an Oxford man, had taken an interest in John Henry's education, and was probably responsible for the last-minute decision to head for Oxford rather than the more scientific and Protestant Cambridge. Mullens' old college, Exeter, had no openings, so John Henry was enrolled at Trinity. Even there, rooms were scarce and it was June before John Henry was able to take up residence, just as the other students were leaving for the long summer vacation. By then he was sixteen, but still some two or three years younger than his classmates. Though he had spent the interval at home in Alton, he was not one to be idle, and had read through an impressive list of Greek and Latin literary works, as well as half of St. Matthew's Gospel in Greek.

Newman's first stay at Oxford was only three weeks—just long enough to count for a term in the lax atmosphere of the pre-reformed university, and just long enough also for the new student, despite his loneliness, to fall in love with the university and its beautiful country town. He bought a gown, and managed to obtain, by his last day, a reading list for the summer. The most important event of these first weeks was meeting John Bowden, a classmate who had been assigned by Newman's tutor to brief Newman on college customs and escort him to dinner on his first night. Bowden, though three years older than Newman, would become his inseparable college companion, and a loyal friend till Bowden's early death in 1844.

Newman applied himself to his studies during his first full year, and he did so well that in the spring his tutor urged him to stand for the college scholarship, though he would be the youngest of the competitors. The exam, which was open to outsiders as well as Trinity men, included Greek and Latin authors, as well as mathematics and an English essay. On May 18ᵗʰ, Trinity Monday, it was announced that Newman had won the competition, and was the new Scholar of Trinity, with a tidy £60 a year for nine years. During that summer of 1818 Newman read some Gibbon, but mostly John Locke on knowledge, and, influenced by the role of the mind in deriving ideas from sense impressions, began to develop his own epistemology, with an emphasis on the personal and subjective dimensions.[2]

The 1818-19 school year found Newman and Bowden publishing an anti-Catholic romance in verse titled *St Bartholomew's Eve* and several issues of an anonymous periodical called *The Undergraduate*. The latter came to a quick end, however, when Newman was too embarrassed to continue it after his involvement became public. During the summer vacation Newman read more Gibbon, and took to imitating his style. He was enthusiastic about the Romanticism of Scott's *Ivanhoe*, but also appreciated the realism and common sense of Crabbe's *Tales of the Hall*. And he continued writing his own verse. Biographer Maisie Ward, a great admirer of Newman's prose, finds him "tone-deaf to poetry," both as a versifier and a reader.[3]

By the next school year Newman and Bowden were deep into preparation for their final examinations, often spending twelve hours a day at their books. Newman, on the wake of his scholarship success, was thinking about a career in law, and became a member of Lincoln's Inn. As the year went by, he became more and more anxious about the final exam, worried that he was reading the wrong books, and concerned that he coveted academic success. The exam dread continued through the summer, while he was alone at Oxford, and into the next school year, as he even increased his reading. The exam week, at the end of November 1820, was a disaster. Though he passed, and earned his B. A., his and others' hopes that he would win high honors were crushed by a decidedly lackluster performance. His fear of failure was fulfilled, his nerves broke, and he went without honors in both math and classics.[4]

Despite the great disappointment, Newman remained steady in failure, and even seemed to gain in maturity and responsibility from it. In a letter to his sister Harriett, he reflected in his Evangelical mode on how his "disappointment was at once a chastisement for former offences, and a kind of preventive of future." As he had worried during the previous year, he was aware that, "among *many* other diseases of the mind, I am very vain, and the least success is apt to alter me,—witness my getting the Trinity Scholarship."[5] Academically, he had learned much from his hard work, in both matter and method, especially from his study of Aristotle's *Ethics*, with its focus on virtues and character, the nature of moral truth, and practical moral judgment.

2. RESPONDING TO A VOCATION

Following the exam fiasco and Christmas holidays, Newman returned to Oxford in February 1821 in good spirits. With the exams behind him, and his Trinity Scholarship good for several more years, he was able to lighten up a bit academically, attending lectures on mineralogy, and expanding his reading in many directions: anatomy, chemistry, and geology; Hebrew, Arabic, and Persian; Plato, Cicero, and Hume. He also had more time now for his music: "Signor Giovanni Enrico Neandrini has finished his first Obiettamento," he announced in a March letter home.[6]

But 1821 was also the year when, in Newman's own words, "he was more devoted to the evangelical creed and more strict in his religious duties than at any previous time." A dream he had in May tells us something about his religious imagination. In it a spirit spoke to him of "the other world": "Among other things it said that it was absolutely impossible for the reason of man to understand the mystery (I think) of the Holy Trinity, and in vain to argue about it; but that every thing in another world was so *very, very plain*, that there was not the slightest difficulty about it." He stressed: "I cannot put into any sufficiently strong form of words the ideas which were conveyed to me. I thought I instantly fell on my knees, overcome with gratitude to God for so kind a message."[7]

During that summer Newman read Evangelical theology and compiled a large collection of scriptural passages, summarizing his beliefs on various themes. Conversion, in particular, puzzled him because his own experience of it did not square with the descriptions in the books. This was also the time when his belief in the Calvinist doctrine of predestination began to fade. Diary entries make it clear that this was a very difficult year in Newman's interior life: distraction and emotional dryness in prayer, sexual temptations, and accusations of pride, vanity, and arrogance fill the records of his self-examinations.[8]

When he returned to Oxford after the summer vacation he moved into out-of-college rooms at a coffeehouse. The family plan was to have his younger brother Francis share lodgings and study with him until Francis entered a college. Like John Henry, Francis had been influenced by the Rev. Mayers during his school years at Ealing, and was at least as strong as John Henry in his Evangelical devotion. It was Francis, in fact, who, with his brother's support, had recently provoked a bad scene with their father by refusing to copy a letter for him on a Sunday. John Henry soon took on a Trinity undergraduate as a private pupil at £100 a year. Unhappily, news came in November that his father's efforts in the brewery business had finally ended in bankruptcy. His father's spirit was crushed, and the family again had to uproot itself. Newman gave sensitive moral support, and more. With prospects of more private pupils, he offered to support Francis' education. And looking for other financial means to help his family, he also hit upon the idea of standing for a Fellowship at the intellectually prestigious Oriel College. Given his exam disappointment, his friends at Trinity thought the idea dangerously unrealistic, simply courting another disaster. But Newman knew he was better than his last exam performance, and thought the attempt, even if unsuccessful, would at least be good practice for a future victory.

Early in January 1822 Newman, home for Christmas vacation, had a conversation with his father after a Sunday church service. Affectionately concerned about his son's religious attitudes and opinions, Mr. Newman took the occasion to caution John Henry in his common sense and very direct way. He had thought, for example, that his son's tone in a published letter to the editor of the *Christian Observer* was "more like the composition of an old man, than of a youth just entering life with energy and aspirations." Newman recorded the substance of his father's warning in his journal that evening, and included a slightly edited version of it in his Memoir five decades later. Because of its importance to Newman, as well as its prophetic insight, this advice of a loving father is worth repeating here. "Take care," he began, "you are encouraging a morbid sensibility and irritability of mind, which may be very serious. Religion, when carried too far, induces a mental softness. No one's principles," he continued, "can be established at twenty." He then pointedly predicted: "Your opinions in two or three years will certainly, certainly change. I have seen many instances of the same kind. You are on dangerous ground. The temper you are encouraging may lead to something alarming. Weak minds are carried into superstition, and strong minds into infidelity;" and he concluded, "do not commit yourself, do nothing ultra."[9] Newman's journal indicates that he took his father's advice to heart. A few days later, just at the end of Christmas vacation, Mr. Newman told John Henry that he should decide on a career. Although the father had envisioned his son in the law, he was satisfied enough with John Henry's choice of the church, a decision the son had already made. Newman, of course, was not just choosing a career, but responding to a vocation. As he set off for Oxford the next day, his father's last words were, again, "Do not show any ultraism in any thing."[10]

On February 21, 1822, Newman wrote in his journal: "My birthday. Today I am of age. It is an awful crisis. I say 'awful,' for it seems to leave me to myself, and I have been as yet used to depend on others." He went on: "May this be a point, from which I may date more decision and firmness in my profession of religion!" He concluded with a short prayer of self-offering: "I am now entering upon a new stage of life, Lord go with me: make me Thy true soldier."[11] When writing to thank his mother for a birthday letter, Newman went a little further: "I seem now more left to myself, and, when I reflect on my own weaknesses, I have cause to shudder." His mother, fearing depression, responded anxiously: "I see one great fault in your character, which alarms me very much, as I observe it increases upon you seriously … . Your fault is want of self confidence, and a dissatisfaction with yourself, that you cannot exceed the bounds of human nature."[12] Newman tried to reassure her that he was in good health, relaxing at many wine and music parties.

3. IMBIBING ORIEL LIBERALISM

The truth, however, was that, with the exam for the Oriel Fellowship approaching, Newman's emotions were anything but steady. His confidence waxed and waned almost daily, and by the exam week his journal consisted mostly of brief reports on his nerves. The Oriel exam put great weight on Latin composition, and the examiners were looking for sharp minds, not just accomplishment. Luckily, during his preparation Newman made a breakthrough on Latin style, discovering the secret of a truly Latin sentence structure; and, of course, he was blessed with acute intelligence. On this occasion both stood him in good stead, and despite a terrible case of nerves and wretched illness, he came from the back of the pack and triumphed over the academic stars of the university. On April 12th, the Friday of this Easter exam week, he was

elected a Fellow of Oriel, fulfilling his greatest dream, but a dream he
had fretted over mightily as it seemed a temptation to pride and vanity.
On that day, "of all days most memorable," Newman took his seat in
the Oriel chapel and dined in the common room, sitting next to John
Keble, the young Fellow commonly acknowledged as the university's
most brilliant star. This day, he later recognized, was the great "turning point of his life." His election "raised him from obscurity and need
to competency and reputation." Theologically, it placed him on "the
high and broad platform of University society and intelligence," and
exposed him to personal and intellectual influences which "gradually
developed and formed" the "religious sentiments in his mind, which
had been his blessing from the time he left school"—from the time,
that is, of his first conversion.[13]

Newman's extreme shyness, now exacerbated by the fame of the
Oriel common room's brilliance, along with his Calvinistic "isolation
of thought and spiritual solitariness,"[14] made the Fellows wonder if his
election had been a blunder. Some of them enlisted Richard Whately,
a former Fellow, to bring Newman out of himself. A great extrovert,
of "generous and warm heart,"[15] Whately was clearly the man for the
job, succeeding, to a degree, in just a few summer months. The independence of mind and action that finally resulted from what Whately
began was, of course, beyond anyone's expectation. Whately got
Newman to assist with his work on logic, but it was mainly through
conversation that he led Newman to "look about" himself and taught
him to "think correctly" and to rely on himself.[16] As Newman put it in
his *Apologia* (1864), he "opened my mind, and taught me to think and
to use my reason"—he "not only taught me to think, but to think for
myself."[17] Whately soon thought Newman was "the clearest-headed
man he knew,"[18] and assured the Fellows that they had made no mistake. Still, Newman did not feel really at home at Oriel for quite a
while, and remained something of a loner. In his *Apologia* he recalled
a day when he was out walking by himself and met the provost, Dr.
Copleston, who courteously bowed and quoted Cicero: "*Nunquam
minus solus, quàm cùm solus.*"[19] This quotation was not to become
Newman's motto, but it might have; it fitted him more perfectly than
even Copleston probably knew.

Newman did not rest on his Oriel laurels. He continued to live with
Francis in lodgings for the next school year, tutored private pupils,
worked hard on the classics, and, thanks to Whately's recommendation,

wrote for the *Encyclopedia Metropolitana*. In April 1823 Newman's probationary year ended successfully with his admission as an actual Fellow, and Edward Pusey, soon to be Newman's great friend and ally, joined him as a new Oriel Fellow. In June Newman began seriously considering how soon he should take holy orders. Toward that end, in November, Newman and Pusey began attending private lectures given by Charles Lloyd, the Regius Professor of Divinity, of the "high-and-dry" school of theology. While the scholarly Lloyd did not "leave a mark upon his [Evangelical] mind,"[20] his brusque manner in the give-and-take of the sessions further helped to draw Newman out of himself.

In May 1824 Newman decided to accept the position of curate at the Oxford working-class parish of St. Clement's, and he was therefore ordained deacon on June 13th. He marked the occasion in his journal: "It is over. I am thine, O Lord … ." With an elderly and incapacitated rector, Newman was soon engaged in intensive pastoral duties, in addition to his academic work. His preaching was appreciated, though some thought he was too severe. This was probably deliberate, as he believed that "Those who make comfort the great subject of their preaching seem to mistake the end of their ministry. *Holiness* is the great end. There must be a struggle and a trial here. Comfort is a cordial, but no one drinks cordials from morning to night." One of his frequent sermon topics was sin. In "Sins against Conscience," he made his favorite, crucial point that conscience must be followed to reach truth.[21]

Newman's new parish duties obligated him to spend the long summer vacation of 1824 in Oxford. This was the occasion for him to develop a close relationship with Oriel Fellow Edward Hawkins, likewise obligated by his duties as Vicar of the University Church, St. Mary's. And this was the beginning of two significant years during which Newman "underwent a great change in his religious opinions, a change brought about by very various influences."[22]

Reviewing these influences in his Memoir, Newman mentions first the great Oriel common room, whose brilliant members were "as remarkable for the complexion of their theology and their union among themselves in it, as for their literary eminence." These Oriel Noetics were neither High Church nor Low Church, but a new school, characterized by "moderation and comprehension." If their enemies were the suspicious "old unspiritual high-and-dry" and the envious members of the smaller and less distinguished colleges, their friends were of the Evangelical party, grateful for the Oriel liberality of mind.[23]

Among these influential members, Hawkins was the most important for Newman at this juncture. During the long vacation he and Newman had the dining hall and common room to themselves, took walks together, and generally spent much time in each other's company, with the older Hawkins as mentor. He taught Newman to weigh his words, to be cautious in his statements, to make clear distinctions—all the mental techniques that formed Newman into a great controversialist.[24] Hawkins also criticized Newman's Evangelical views, which, as Newman later admitted, he took for granted rather than held intelligently. Central here, of course, was the Evangelical teaching on the nature and primacy of personal, consciously experienced conversion as *the* grace-filled saving event in the life of the elect. For example, when Newman showed him his first sermon, Hawkins came down hard on its implied denial of baptismal regeneration. Hawkins told Newman that it is impossible to draw a line, as his sermon did, between "two classes, the one all darkness, the other all light," because "moral and religious excellence is a matter of degree. Men are not either saints or sinners; but they are not so good as they should be, and better than they might be,—more or less converted to God … ." Preachers, he said, "should follow the example of St Paul; *he* did not divide his brethren into two, the converted and unconverted, but he addressed them all as 'in Christ' … ." Hawkins had this view from John Sumner's *Apostolical Preaching* (1815), which he gave to Newman. This book, according to Newman, was finally successful, "beyond any thing else, in routing out evangelical doctrines" from his creed,[25] and leading him to accept the doctrine of baptismal regeneration.[26]

But this change did not come easily. In a journal entry for August 24, 1824 we see the pain in Newman's conscience as he struggled for the truth. "Sumner's book threatens to drive me either into Calvinism, or baptismal regeneration, and I wish to steer clear of both … . I am always slow in deciding a question; but last night I was so distressed and low about it, that … the thought even struck me I must leave the Church. I have been praying about it," he continued, and "I do not know what will be the end of it. I think I really desire the truth, and would embrace it wherever I found it." Five months later (January 13, 1825), he was still struggling, but with more clarity. "I think, I am not certain, I must give up the doctrine of imputed righteousness and that of regeneration as apart from baptism." Continuing, he explained, "It seems to me that the great stand is to be made, *not* against those who connect a spiritual change with baptism, but those who deny a spiritual change altogether.... . All who confess the natural corruption of the heart, and the necessity of a change," he went on, "should unite against those who make it (regeneration) a mere opening of new prospects, when the old score of offences is wiped away, and a person is for the second time put, as it were, on his good behaviour." Among the reasons he lists favoring this view is that "it seems more agreeable to the analogy of God's works, that there should be no harsh line, but degrees of holiness indefinitely small." If the reference to analogy sounds Catholic, decades later, as a Roman Catholic, Newman reflected on the radicality of these ideas in his Memoir: "Here he had in fact got hold of the Catholic doctrine that forgiveness of sin is conveyed to us, not simply by imputation, but by the implanting of a habit of grace."[27]

This critical questioning of his Evangelical beliefs on the intellectual level was supported on the experiential level not only by his personal experience of conversion, which as he had discovered did not conform to the Evangelical model, but also by his pastoral work. Indeed, in his parish duties Newman "found as a fact" what Hawkins had told him— that "Calvinism was not a key to the phenomena of human nature, as they occur in the world." Evangelical teaching was "unreal," it "would not work in a parish." This empirical sense appears in his journal a few months later: "I may add to my ... remarks on my change of sentiment as to Regeneration, that I have been principally or in a great measure led to this change by the fact that in my parochial duties I found many, who in most important points were inconsistent, but whom yet I could not say were altogether without grace. Most indeed were in that condition as if they had some spiritual feelings, but were weak and uncertain." So, with his own experience reinforcing Hawkins' advice, Newman, "before many months of his clerical life were over, had," as he put it in his Memoir, "taken the first steps towards giving up the evangelical form of Christianity ... ."[28]

On September 29, 1824 Newman's father died at age fifty-nine. Newman had arrived home for his father's last few days, when "He seemed in great peace of mind," despite his financial ruin. Newman was now the man of the family. The death occasioned a journal musing: "When I die, shall I be followed to the grave by my children? my Mother said the other day she hoped to live to see me married, but

I think I shall either die within a College walls, or a Missionary in a foreign land—no matter where, so that I die in Christ."[29]

Hawkins was not the only important influence on Newman. After his election in October 1824 as junior treasurer of Oriel, which brought welcome additional income, Newman was appointed by Whately, now principal of Alban Hall, a small university residence, as his vice-principal (dean, tutor, bursar, etc.), in March 1825. This put him again in close contact with Whately, and exposed to his ideas, which had "a gradual, but deep effect" on his mind. In his *Apologia*, Newman put Whately's influence this way: "What he did for me in point of religious opinion, was, first, to teach me the existence of the Church, as a substantive body or corporation; next to fix in me those anti-Erastian views of Church polity, which were [in the next decade to become] one of the most prominent features of the Tractarian movement." For Newman this principally meant the mutual independence of church and state; the church's right to retain its property; and the state's entitlement to the church's support.[30]

In 1825 Newman read Bishop Joseph Butler's *Analogy of Religion* (1736), with its "inculcation of a visible Church, the oracle of truth and a pattern of sanctity, of the duties of external religion, and of the historical character of Revelation … ." Two of Butler's points especially influenced him, and became fundamental principles of his thought, as he later explained in his *Apologia*. "First, the very idea of an analogy between the separate works of God leads to the conclusion that the system which is of less importance is economically or sacramentally connected with the more momentous system, and of this conclusion the theory, to which I was inclined as a boy, viz. the unreality of material phenomena, is an ultimate resolution." Then, to analogy Newman adds probability. "Secondly, Butler's doctrine that Probability is the guide of life, led me, at least under the teaching to which a few years later I was introduced, to the question of the logical cogency of Faith … ."[31] These ideas, he later thought, placed "his doctrinal views on a broad philosophical basis, with which an emotional religion could have little sympathy."[32]

In the *Apologia* Newman acknowledged two further influences from the Oriel common room. The Reverend William James taught him the doctrine of apostolical succession, though he was "impatient" with it at the time, and the former Roman Catholic priest Joseph Blanco White introduced him to "freer views on the subject of inspiration than were usual in the Church of England at the time."[33] But it was Hawkins and Whately who had the greatest impact on Newman's thinking in these years, so we should return to them to complete this survey of Oriel influences. When Newman was an undergraduate he had heard Hawkins preach a university sermon on tradition, a sermon Whately had encouraged him to give. Now, as a Fellow himself, Newman read and studied the sermon very carefully, and was greatly impressed by its "*quasi*-Catholic doctrine of Tradition, as a main element in ascertaining and teaching the truths of Christianity."[34] It asserted the basic point that "the sacred text was never intended to teach doctrine, but only to prove it, and that, if we would learn doctrine, we must have recourse to the formularies of the Church; for instance to the Catechism, and to the Creeds." This view, "most true in its outline, most fruitful in its consequences," opened a "large field of thought" for Newman.[35]

Newman was ordained to the priesthood on the feast of Pentecost, May 29, 1825. His journal entry for that day reflected considerably less spiritual condescension toward his fellow ordinands than it had the previous year, when, in his narrowly Evangelical view as to who counted as a real Christian, he had harshly judged some to be "coming to the Bishop ... without the Spirit of God."[36] He now held the more generous presumption in favor of Christians being in the kingdom of grace by virtue of baptism. In Meriol Trevor's judgment, Newman had made the shift "from a subjective to an objective view of the scheme of salvation" by the time of his ordination.[37] In other words, Newman had by this time dropped the Evangelical insistence on the once-and-for-all subjective experience of conversion, with its assurance of salvation, and moved to a view of sanctification as more gradual and objectively linked to baptism.

In his 1874 Memoir Newman made it clear that, despite all the good it had done for him, Evangelicalism was never really right for him. Yes, it had converted him to a spiritual life, but the "peculiarities of evangelical religion had never been congenial to him," he wrote, "though he had fancied he held them. Its emotional and feverish devotion and its tumultuous experiences were foreign to his nature, which indeed was ever conspicuously faulty in the opposite direction, as being in a way incapable, as if physically, of enthusiasm, however legitimate and guarded." He also cited his great attraction to the Greek and Latin classics and to the Fathers as another reason why "the ethical character of the Evangelical Religion could not lastingly be imprinted" on his mind.[38] In short, though just what he needed at fifteen, Evangelicalism was not, in the final analysis, a good fit for Newman.

4. CHECKING THE DRIFT TOWARD LIBERALISM

But if Newman had escaped "the crags and precipices of Luther and Calvin" by the time he was ordained a priest, where was he to go? The likely refuge was the "flats" of a cold Arminian doctrine, at the time "the intellectual and ecclesiastical antagonist and alternative of the Evangelical creed … ."[39] And, indeed, Newman, influenced by the Liberalism of the Oriel common room, headed in that direction. Typical of people in transitional phases, he had lost his firm cognitive bearings. Expanding the metaphor a bit, we may say that Newman had left a secure Evangelical port and now, sailing on a cloudy night without an intellectual compass, found himself seized by a strong Liberal current, named, from different perspectives, Rationalist or Latitudinarian. For example, in preparation for an encyclopedia article on miracles, he read Hume, and was particularly impressed by the equally skeptical Conyers Middleton.[40] In his correspondence with his youngest brother, Charles, now an atheist, Newman argued the then rather radical anti-literalist view that "the New Testament is not Christianity, but the *record* of Christianity,"[41] and any problems in the books do not overthrow the faith they record. But he also argued that rejection of Christianity arises "from a fault of the *heart*, not of the *intellect*," that a "dislike of the *contents* of Scripture is at the bottom of unbelief."[42] And in the *Apologia*, he turned this last argument against himself. "The truth is," he wrote, "I was beginning to prefer intellectual excellence to moral; I was drifting in the direction of the Liberalism of the day. I was rudely awakened from my dream at the end of 1827 by two great blows—illness and bereavement."[43]

Everything seemed to be going well. Early in 1826 Newman had been appointed an Oriel tutor, the position he much desired. His *Metropolitana* articles had been well received. He preached his first university sermon, and began to be known. In 1827, he was appointed a public examiner for the B.A. degree. He had, as he put it in the *Apologia*, come out of his shell and "began to have influence."[44]

But, then, in late November 1827, exactly seven years after failing to gain honors in his own exams, everything fell to pieces as he was conducting his first public examination. Suddenly he found his "memory and mind gone," and could not continue.[45] Several external pressures had been aggravated, as seven years earlier, by extreme overwork and worry in his preparation for the exams. He was confused, unable to think, and his brain and eyes seemed twisted. After consulting a doctor and being leached on his temples, he left Oxford, finally joining his family in Brighton.

He had hardly recovered when, suddenly, while he was still at home just six weeks later, his greatly loved youngest sister, Mary, only nineteen, took ill at dinner and, after a night of violent spasms, died the next day, January 5, 1828. Newman was devastated. His journal entry thirteen weeks later called Mary's death "the heaviest affliction with which the good hand of God has ever visited me."[46] One major effect of Mary's death on Newman was a more intense intuition of an invisible, but more real, world hidden behind this world. He expressed this heightened supernatural sense in a letter to his sister Jemima a few months after Mary's death, relating how, as he rode through the green countryside, "Dear Mary seems embodied in every tree and hid behind every hill. What a veil and curtain this world of sense is! beautiful but still a veil."[47] To such intensely personal blows no merely intellectual response could be adequate. They shook Newman from his Liberalism, and set him on a new religious course, fortified, beyond rational logic and common sense, with the richly imaginative power of metaphor. As Whately and Hawkins had been his guides out of Evangelicalism, he would have new companions for the next part of his journey, principally, Edward Pusey, R. Hurrell Froude, and John Keble.[48]

5. TURNING TOWARD HIGH CHURCH THEOLOGY

Edward Pusey had been elected to an Oriel Fellowship in April 1823, one year after Newman. Both were scholarly and religious, and they bonded immediately, though Pusey had little sympathy for Newman's Evangelical views. They talked constantly about religion, and participated in Lloyd's theological sessions the following school year. Newman's journal entries reflected a growing appreciation of Pusey's depth of character, despite their theological differences. His entry for December 16, 1824 indicates Pusey's theological influence: "I am lodged in the same house with Pusey, and we have had many talks on the subject of religion, I arguing for imputed righteousness, he against it, I inclining to separate regeneration from baptism, he doubting its separation &c." This was less than a month before Newman wrote

(January 13, 1825) as already noted: "I think, I am not certain, I must give up the doctrine of imputed righteousness and that of regeneration as apart from baptism." A year later (February 21, 1826), he wrote: "I am almost convinced against predestination and election in the Calvinistic sense, that is, I see no proof of them in Scripture." He immediately added an intriguing comment: "Pusey accused me the other day of becoming more High Church."[49] Pusey himself was soon off to Göttingen and Berlin to study German theology, but their important relationship continued. On his return in 1827, he brought Newman a collection of the Fathers.

In March 1826 R. Hurrell Froude had been elected a Fellow of Oriel. Newman immediately found him "one of the acutest and clearest and deepest men in the memory of man,"[50] and they eventually became the greatest of friends. Froude's father was a traditional High Church archdeacon, and Froude himself was an uncompromising High Churchman, more enchanted with the medieval church than with the Reformers.[51] When they first met, Froude was put off by what was left of Newman's Evangelical views as well as by the Liberalism Newman was then flirting with. But Froude would soon deal with what he saw as Newman's heresies. Though Froude's personality was complex, with a definitely dark side,[52] Newman, in the *Apologia*, rhapsodized about his gentle, playful, graceful character, and praised him as "a man of high genius," overflowing with original ideas, possessed of an "intellect as critical and logical as it was speculative and bold." While Froude had "no turn for theology as such," Newman described him as "an Englishman to the backbone in his severe adherence to the real and the concrete," but with "a keen insight into abstract truth."[53] Newman was clearly impressed.

Almost four decades later, in his *Apologia*, Newman summarized Froude's influence on him: "He taught me to look with admiration towards the Church of Rome, and in the same degree to dislike the Reformation. He fixed deep in me the idea of devotion to the Blessed Virgin, and he led me gradually to believe in the Real Presence."[54] All of this was combined with a high regard for tradition and a scorn for the idea of scripture alone. This influence was spread over a decade, till Froude's early death in 1836, and it is difficult to say exactly how much of it was present in the late 1820s. But Newman did invoke Froude's authority as early as March 1828 as he argued "for lowering the intellectual powers into hand-maids of our moral nature," intellect being subordinate to something more fundamental in us. "Each mind," he wrote, "pursues its own course and is actuated in that course by tenthousand indescribable incommunicable feelings and imaginings. It would be comparatively easy to enumerate the various external impulses which determine the capricious motions of a floating feather or web, ... so mysterious are the paths of thought."[55] Also from 1828, Newman relates a key event which he quotes from Froude's *Remains*: "Do you know the story of the murderer who had done one good thing in his life? Well, if I was ever asked what good deed I had ever done, I should say that I had brought Keble and Newman to understand each other."[56] This brings us to the other great personal influence on Newman—John Keble.

Newman had first met Keble in the Oriel common room the day Newman was elected Fellow in 1822. Newman was tongue-tied on that occasion. Keble was not then in residence, so Newman saw little of him. In retrospect, Newman thought that Keble was "shy" of him for years because of Newman's Evangelical and Liberal perspectives.[57] In 1828 a new provost needed to be elected at Oriel; Hawkins and Keble were the candidates. Newman favored his mentor Hawkins, who was, in fact, successful. But the election campaign was the occasion for Froude to sing the praises of his former teacher Keble, and Newman "became conscious for the first time of his own congeniality of mind with Keble."[58] With Hawkins now provost, Newman succeeded him as Vicar of the University Church, St. Mary the Virgin, on March 14, 1828.

Keble's collection of sacred verse, *The Christian Year*, had appeared in 1827. As Newman looked back at the volume's impact on him, he wrote that he could not pretend to analyze "the effect of religious teachings so deep, so pure, so beautiful." He did emphasize, however, that it reinforced "the two main intellectual truths" which he had learned from Butler, now creatively recast by his "new master": the sacramental system (analogy) and probability. The first, the sacramental idea in the large sense, is "the doctrine that material phenomena are both the types and the instruments of real things unseen ... ." The second is the claim that in matters religious, "it is not merely probability which makes us intellectually certain, but probability as it is put to account by faith and love ... which give to probability a force which it has not in itself." As much as he agreed with this "beautiful and religious" view of probability, Newman was dissatisfied because it was not logical enough, "it did not go to the root of the difficulty." He would later try to improve it in various works, including, of course, his *Essay in Aid of a Grammar of Assent* (1870). In his *Apologia*, he capsulized his basic argument this way: "that that absolute certitude which we were able to possess, whether as to the truths of natural theology, or as to the fact of a revelation, was the result of an *assemblage* of concurring and converging probabilities, and that, both according to the constitution of the human mind and the will of its Maker ... ."[59]

After his first conversion in 1816, Newman had become "enamoured" of the great Early Christian writers, especially Augustine and Ambrose, learned from extracts in Milner's *History*. However, this early interest waned over the next decade to the point "of a certain disdain for Antiquity," which "showed itself in some flippant language against the Fathers" in his contribution to the *Encyclopedia Metropolitana*. As he now "moved out of the shadow" of Liberalism, that interest revived, and in the summer of 1828 he started reading the Fathers chronologically, beginning with Ignatius and Justin. Before long he was developing the idea "that Antiquity was the true exponent of the doctrines of Christianity and the basis of the Church of England." He was particularly attracted to the Alexandrians. Later he wrote: "Some portions of their teaching, magnificent in themselves, came like music to my inner ear, as if the response to ideas, which, with little external to encourage them, I had cherished so long." These teachings were "based on the mystical or sacramental principle," which he understood "to mean that the exterior world, physical and historical, was but the manifestation to our senses of realities greater than itself." He extended this idea both to the entire history of salvation and to such specific topics as angels and other preternatural creatures.[60]

Despite Newman's affection and respect for Hawkins, and his enthusiastic support of his candidacy for provost, two events—important in Newman's development—damaged their relationship soon after Hawkins became provost.

First, Newman and Hawkins split on the question of Robert Peel's re-election to Parliament, brought on by the issue of Catholic emancipation. In February 1829 the university passed a petition against emancipation by a large majority. Though Newman had no strong political view on the issue, he was adamantly opposed to the re-election of Peel, who, as a Tory representing the university, had reversed his position by declaring himself in favor of emancipation, resigned, and was now standing for re-election. Newman saw him as an unprincipled "rat." Hawkins, without consulting the Oriel Fellows, threw his support behind Peel. Newman had previously, under Whately's influence, been among the minority in the university favoring Catholic emancipation. Now his religious opposition to emancipation, seen as a Liberal cause, reflected the growing influence of Keble and Froude, and the diminishment of Whately's. Evidently, a change of mind was acceptable for an Oriel Fellow, but not for a Member of Parliament. Though Peel's loss was a victory for Newman, the most important result for Newman was his loss of trust in Hawkins.

Second, Newman and Hawkins disagreed on the nature of an Oriel tutorship, with Newman favoring maximum attention to the most promising students. Even before Hawkins became provost, Newman, viewing his tutorial position as a ministerial vocation, had begun reorganizing the tutor-student relationship. Basically, he and his fellow tutors arranged to deal with indifferent, uninterested students, the majority, in large lectures, leaving more time to work individually and in small groups with the more promising students aiming at honors. After Hawkins had been provost for a time, he began to oppose this approach, maintaining that "Newman was sacrificing the many to the few, and governing, not by intelligible rules and their impartial application, but by a system, if it was so to be called, of mere personal influence and favoritism."[61] For Newman, having a pastoral relationship with special pupils was a matter of principle, and he refused to go back to the old system of treating all students alike. After much fruitless negotiation, Hawkins finally laid down the law in June 1830, letting Newman and his fellow tutors know that they would be given no new students, effectively ending their positions as their present students graduated. Newman's great hopes for Oriel under Hawkins thus ended in deep disappointment. Only in retrospect would Newman realize that this end of his tutorship made possible the next great phase of his life—the Tractarian Movement of the 1830s. But that is a story for another chapter. More immediately, the decrease in Newman's tutorial responsibilities freed him up for two new opportunities—a book and a trip.

First, in March 1831, Hugh James Rose, co-editor of a new library of theological works, invited Newman to write a history of church councils. Newman accepted, but, during the next year of writing, so changed the original conception that the result, *The Arians of the*

Fourth Century, was rejected by the editors as inappropriate for the theological library, though published separately. Newman saw important similarities between Arianism and the religious Liberalism of his day, both guilty, in his view, of an erroneous subjection of revelation to human reason. Here, also, related to his analogical and sacramental thinking, Newman explained the early church's principle of economy, whereby Divine Truth was reserved and dispensed in stages and degrees by various means (nature, pagan religion, philosophy, scriptures) appropriate to the preparation of the recipient. And it was in this first book, too, as Ian Ker points out, that Newman was already anticipating his important epistemological identification of the true and the real, defining "the true and the false in terms of the real and the unreal."[62]

Newman finished *The Arians* just in time to meet his July 1832 deadline, leaving him free to consider the second opportunity, an invitation from Froude to join him and his father on an extended Mediterranean trip. He decided to go, and they set sail from Falmouth on December 8th. Over the next months they visited Gibraltar, Malta, Corfu, Naples, Sicily, and Rome. His travel experiences caused Newman to revise his thinking about the unreformed churches, especially the Roman Catholic Anti-Christ, and he worked at distinguishing the Catholic from its Roman corruption. Newman was especially captivated by the beauty of Sicily, and, in early April, when the Froudes departed for home, he set out by himself to visit Sicily again. Before too many days of primitive conditions in Sicily Newman fell seriously ill with a fever at the beginning of May, and spent most of the month in precarious health, at one point being feared near death. Years later, writing in his 1874 Memoir, Newman regarded this experience as the last of his three great illnesses, all linked to critical moments in his religious life.[63] A few years after the illness, Newman wrote that he thought the devil had tried to do him in to keep him from the upcoming battles.[64] But he knew that God had other plans. When he was finally recovered and ready to travel again, he sat by his bed one morning, crying bitterly: "all I could say was, that I was sure God had some work for me to do in England."[65] Newman reached England on July 8th, just as Keble was about to fire from the university pulpit what Newman regarded as the opening shot of the Oxford war, the Assize Sermon on National Apostasy.[66]

6. COGNITIVE CONVERSION

What was going on in Newman's knowing during these dozen years? Did he experience a cognitive conversion as he moved from Evangelical to Liberal to High Church theology? We can begin an answer by re-calling the distinction between content (what) and structure (how).

First, in terms of *content*, it is clear that Newman underwent a major change in his views or beliefs during these years. We have noted how he was influenced by Whately (and Butler) on his understanding of church, by Hawkins on tradition, and by James on apostolical succes-sion and White on inspiration. Perhaps the most important doctri-nal change during this period was in Newman's shift, influenced by Hawkins (Sumner) and Pusey, from regarding a personal experience of conversion as necessary for salvation to an acceptance of baptis-mal regeneration. Though more difficult to pin down exactly in terms of time, we also noted the general influence of Froude's preference of Rome over the Reformation. There were other important changes in *what* Newman thought: for example, the crucial epistemological views of Butler and Keble on analogy and probability, and the lessons from Locke and Aristotle on the nature of knowledge and morality. Though surely matters of content, these are better understood as changes in the *how* of Newman's knowing, to which we now turn.

When we consider change in the *structural* shape of Newman's knowing, there are several aspects to examine. In the next few para-graphs we will attend to structural transformation from the following angles: subjective/objective; independent judgment; empirical/ideal; and emotional/rational.

Newman's recognition of the *subjective*, personal dimension of knowing, learned from his study of Locke, was nicely complemented by Butler and Keble's stress on probability and by Aristotle's under-standing of moral judgment, both of which involve the grasp of mean-ing in concrete situations through personal insight. At the same time, his thinking, as Trevor points out in relation to baptism, was becom-ing more *objective*. Though his theology was not systematic in the ordi-nary sense, he was becoming more systematic in his thinking. Greater subjectivity results in greater objectivity.

The key issue of *independent judgment* is also complex with Newman. Although he explains that Whately taught him to think for himself, it is clear that personal influences remained very important for him—not only Whately and Hawkins, but also Pusey, Froude, and Keble. Indeed, the latter trio influenced him away from the views (and eventually even the friendship) of the first pair. Newman's critical independence of mind was growing, but it was still far from complete at this point. As in other aspects of his knowing, there was a decided ambivalence here.

Newman's undergraduate study of Aristotle and Locke made a definite and central impact on the *empirical/ideal* aspect. Both authors contributed much to Newman's appreciation of the empirical dimension of knowing. This empirical emphasis was an important counterbalance to a cognitive idealism that had dominated his childhood. In his *Apologia* Newman included some childhood memories he had recorded as a young man (1820). He recalled that he was "very superstitious," and that his "imagination ran on unknown influences, on magical powers, and talismans," adding: "I thought life might be a dream, or I an Angel, and all this world a deception, my fellow-angels by a playful device concealing themselves from me, and deceiving me with the semblance of a material world." Newman also recalled in his *Apologia* that the belief in final perseverance involved in his first conversion at age fifteen had directed his mind along the lines of his childhood fantasies: "in isolating me from the objects which surrounded me, in confirming me in my mistrust of the reality of material phenomena, and making me rest in the thought of two and two only absolute and luminously self-evident beings, myself and my Creator ... ."[67] Despite the later empirical influence, this idealistic dimension remained, and surfaced clearly, as we noted, in Newman's reaction to his sister Mary's death in 1828. The intuition of an invisible world, more real than the visible, was a definite aspect of *how* he knew—his alleged English Platonism.[68] With this tension between the empirical and the ideal, it is easy to appreciate how the analogical (sacramental) views of Butler and Keble appealed so strongly to Newman, as they allowed him the possibility of integrating these two basic tendencies of his knowing.

In the next decade Newman would develop his famous *Via Media* argument justifying Anglo-Catholicism in relation to the extremes of Romanism and Protestantism. But here, in the 1820s, he anticipated the structure of this ecclesiological *Via Media* in an important epistemological *via media*. After years of struggling with the cognitive extremes of *emotional* Evangelical religion on the one hand, and Liberal *Rationalism* on the other, he finally found a satisfying *via media* in the patristic use of images, symbols, and analogy. This is the same insight that resolved his empirical/ideal tension. Thus, in one insight he solved his two key epistemological dilemmas. Confirming his basic childhood intuition of a really real invisible world of the supernatural, this epistemological *via media*, unlike the later *Via Media*, was a middle way he would follow for the rest of his life.

At the end of the 1820s it was not clear where this new way would take him, but it is now clear that Newman had made a definite turn in both the content and structure of his knowing, a significant cognitive conversion. Because his understanding of probability needed greater nuance, because his independence of mind was less than firm, and because his resolution of the tension between the empirical and the ideal was more imaginative than critical, still tied to the invisible world of his childhood fantasies in a supernatural realism, Newman's cognitive conversion of the 1820s, though real, was less than completely adequate. But the most important point is certain: the moral commitment of Newman's first conversion at age fifteen was definitively expanded into a radical search for truth through this cognitive transformation in his twenties. His conscience had found true north; there remained the excruciating labor of charting and following his journey's course.[69] Before we continue tracing that journey, we will consider in the final section of this chapter Newman's fuller personal development, beginning with the issue of identity.

7. IDENTITY AND YOUNG ADULT DEVELOPMENT

Erik Erikson understands *identity* as both individual and social. It includes a (sometimes intense) subjective sense of continuity as an active, alive individual who exists in a community with traditional values. Development involves the individual and community sharing mutual relevance and significance.

In chapter 1 we saw the foundation of Newman's identity established in his basic Christian moral conversion at age fifteen. That conversion integrated his previous identifications in a commitment of fidelity to value that transcended his earlier sense of self. Now we have seen this fundamental identity become stronger and more fully defined through many experiences in Newman's early adulthood. On his twenty-first birthday in 1822 Newman recognized that he had come of age and was entering a new stage of life, a stage of independence. Spiritually, he marked the occasion this way: "May this be a point, from which I

may date more decision and firmness in my profession of religion."[70]
We noted how Whately and others fostered Newman's sense of independence. His father's death in 1824 clearly defined Newman as the
man of the family. By 1827 he sensed that he had come out of his shell
and was making his mark in the world.[71]

With a solid sense of identity established, a meaningful kind of *intimacy* is possible. In Erikson's view, a consolidated identity permits
the self-abandonment required not only by passionate sexual relationships, but also by intimate affiliations and inspiring encounters.[72]
Though Newman's calling to a single life precluded explicit sexual
union, inspiring affiliations marked his young adulthood. The specific psychosocial strength of this period is love (for Newman, love
of family, friends, parishioners, students).[73] We saw Newman's developing intimacy not only with older mentoring figures like Whately
and Hawkins, but especially with contemporaries like Pusey, Froude,
and Keble. It would be difficult to overestimate the importance of
Newman's relationships with these mentors and friends. They all
played major roles in making Newman who he became, despite the
problems involved with replacing the first pair with the latter trio.

Though love is secured in intimacy, for Erikson it finds its fulfillment
only in *generativity*. This concerns establishing and guiding the next
generation through caring responsibility, but it also means productiv-
ity and creativity. During his twenties Newman began what would
become a lifelong gushing stream of letters and publications, through
which he poured himself out. We have also noted how Newman took
responsibility for his brother Francis' education at Oxford, and how
deeply he loved and, after his father's death, effectively cared for his
entire family. After his ordination Newman also devoted great time
and energy to the spiritual care of his parishioners. But the most important realization of generativity in this early adult period was clearly
Newman's devotion to his students during his years as tutor at Oriel.
This was the position he had dreamed of, and that he loved so much.
But his rigid understanding of the tutorship as primarily a pastoral
relationship with select students aiming at honors finally cost him the
opportunity of continuing as tutor after only a half dozen years.

Erikson's generativity leads us directly to Kohlberg's highest *postconventional* stages of moral reasoning. Along with advanced critical, reflective cognitive ability, experience of responsible caring is for
Kohlberg a necessary condition for development to a postconventional

orientation. In Newman's movement to a more personal, independent, empirical, and integrated cognitive stance, we can see a shift, in Piagetian terms, from the adolescent's abstract, idealistic thinking toward the adult's contextual, realistic knowing. While far from complete, this shift laid the foundation for at least the beginning of a transition in Newman from conventional to postconventional moral reasoning. For Kohlberg, a fully postconventional orientation is characterized by autonomous moral reasoning in accord with self-chosen universal ethical principles. We saw the independence of autonomous moral reasoning, though perhaps not the universality of ethical principles, in the stand Newman took for his understanding of the tutor-student relationship, even though it meant going against Hawkins, his friend and mentor (and eventually losing his cherished tutorship).

Like the transition from conventional to postconventional moral reasoning, the shift from Fowler's Stage 3 *Synthetic-Conventional* faith to Stage 4 *Individuative-Reflective* faith involves a major breakthrough. In faithing, it is a breakthrough to a new self-awareness and personal responsibility for one's commitments, life-style, beliefs, and attitudes. All of this seems clearly present during Newman's twenties, as he was ordained, assumed pastoral responsibilities, and moved deliberately, though painfully, from Evangelical, through Liberal, to High Church theology. The picture is more complicated, however, with Fowler's Stage 5 *Conjunctive (Paradoxical-Consolidative)* faith, in which symbolic knowing and integration of the "other" are central dimensions. Newman, especially through the influence of Butler, Keble, and the early Christian writers, had come to appreciate the importance of symbolic knowing. Symbols, as we have seen, helped Newman to resolve the basic tension between the cognitive extremes of emotional Evangelicalism and Liberal rationalism. Still, though symbols became a significant content of Newman's knowing, the degree to which he held them in a post-critical rather than pre-critical manner is less clear. Wherever the truth may lie on that question, the other key dimension of Stage 5 faithing, integration of the "other," is especially problematic with Newman. For Fowler, what Stage 4 needs to exclude, Stage 5 manages to include. A central aspect of Stage 4 faithing is the struggle to discover and delineate one's own individuality, and initially this involves defining oneself over against others. During his twenties, at least, Newman was far too involved in this struggle of discovering his own truth to be able to recognize and honor the truth in others' positions. Given the complexity of the religious world he was searching in, Newman needed to exclude. So, despite his important discovery of symbols, it seems safe to conclude that at this period Newman was faithing in Stage 4, not Stage 5.

When we bring all these developmental threads together, and ask about the fabric of Newman's *self* during his twenties, we see a solidly, if not completely, established Stage 4 *Institutional* self. Kegan defines this stage in terms of the self's differentiation from its relationships in the creation of a coherent identity of its own throughout the interpersonal context. No longer merely *being* its relationships, the self now *has* them, relativized within the psychic institution that regulates them. As a result, the self now has a sense of self-ownership. We saw evidence of a shift to this fourth stage of self not only in the resolution of Newman's identity crisis in his adolescent conversion, but also in the consolidation of his identity in various experiences throughout his twenties.

So, by his early thirties, we have a Newman in clear possession of himself—of his cognitive powers, of his identity, of his moral consciousness, of his faith. Or so it seems. He was definitely still struggling with the intimacy and generativity of relationships, as we saw in his difficulties with Hawkins, his friend, mentor, and provost. As we shall soon see, Newman's struggle with the "other"—friend and foe alike—had actually just begun.

3. FROM OXFORD TRACTARIAN
TO ROMAN CONVERT

I. THE JOURNEY FROM OXFORD TO ROME

On July 8, 1833 John Henry Newman returned to England, energized and ready for battle. Though he had been on the Mediterranean trip for exactly seven full months, England had never been far from his mind. In a sense, the journey had served as a retreat for Newman to prepare himself for the challenge of defending the church against its enemies. In particular, the vocational intensification accompanying his serious illness in Sicily had focused him for political battle. On the return voyage he had expressed his openness to God's direction in "Lead, Kindly Light." The Irish Church Reform Bill, which would abolish ten sees and impose a tax on clerical incomes to support the church, was only the most blatant of recent Liberal moves which Newman and his friends saw as undermining the proper status, independence, and authority of the established church. Instead of the threatened external parliamentary reform of the church, Newman saw the need for true inner reform by the church of itself— a second reformation, an Anglican counter reformation returning to the principles of the seventeenth century rather than the sixteenth. In his *Apologia* Newman recalled that "The following Sunday, July 14th, Mr. Keble preached the Assize Sermon [against the Reform Bill] in the University Pulpit. It was published under the title of 'National Apostasy.' I have ever considered and kept the day, as the start of the religious movement of 1833."[1] Newman, indeed, looked first to Keble for leadership.

THE MOVEMENT BEGINS

A meeting was held at Hadleigh before the month was out, and, to rally the clerical troops, a society was formed at Oxford, with a focus on apostolic succession, defense of the Prayer Book, and opposition to "heretical" church appointments.[2] But Newman's strategic thinking went more to bold, lone sharp shooters than to a line of ecclesiastical Red Coats, and when he began editing the *Tracts for the Times* they were the works of individual authors, not of a committee. Thus, when the first *Tract*, on apostolic succession, appeared in September, it came from Newman's own hand. In addition to his labors on the *Tracts*, Newman was fully engaged in spreading the Movement's work—writing letters and visiting clergy around the country. At its start the Movement included members of all parts of the established church, except for Liberals: not only Newman's Apostolicals, but also the "high and dry" and even the Evangelicals. In August the *British Magazine* had begun publishing Newman's "Letters on the Church of the Fathers," with the first focused on St. Ambrose and the power of the people in the church. The Movement's literary arsenal also included the *Lyra Apostolica* in verse, stories of the Apostles and Fathers in "Records of the Church," and a series of letters by Newman on "Church Reform" in the *Record*, which came to an abrupt end when the editor refused to publish the sixth—a clear sign of the building opposition to the Movement. But Newman had already fired another key shot in November with the publication of the *Arians*. A wider, more organized, and thus eventually watered-down effort was the collection of some 7,000 signatures for an Address to the Archbishop of Canterbury, presented early in 1834 supporting him and the church. Early 1834 also saw the appearance of the first volume of Newman's *Parochial and Plain Sermons*. Originally preached to his parishioners at St. Mary's, these sermons were matched in importance for the Movement only by the *Tracts*. They centrally featured the indwelling of the Holy Spirit, which, as Ker stresses, was "at the heart of the new Tractarian emphasis on 'mystery' as opposed to the 'enthusiasm' of Evangelicals and the 'coldness' and 'dryness' of the liberal and high-and-dry Anglicans."[3]

NEWMAN'S POSITION: THREE PROPOSITIONS

In his *Apologia* Newman summarized in three propositions the "position" he held at the beginning of the Movement. "First," he writes, "was the principle of dogma: my battle was with liberalism; by liberalism I mean the anti-dogmatic principle and its developments. This was the first point on which I was certain." In a second edition he further explained his understanding of Liberalism as a "false liberty of thought." It is "the mistake of subjecting to human judgment those revealed doctrines which are in their nature beyond and independent of it, and of claiming to determine on intrinsic grounds the truth and value of propositions which rest for their reception simply on the external authority of the Divine Word." On this first point of dogma, Newman writes: "I have changed in many things: in this I have not. From the age of fifteen, dogma has been the fundamental principle of my religion: I know no other religion; I cannot enter into the idea of any other sort of religion; religion, as a mere sentiment, is to me a dream and a mockery." He then specifies: "As well can there be filial love without the fact of a father, as devotion without the fact of a Supreme Being." He concludes: "What I held in 1816, I held in 1833, and I hold in 1864. Please God, I shall hold it to the end." Dogma, Newman flatly asserts, was "the fundamental principle of the Movement of 1833."[4]

"Secondly," Newman writes in his *Apologia*, "I was confident in the truth of a certain definite religious teaching, based on this foundation of dogma; viz. that there was a visible Church [of Episcopal system] with sacraments and rites which are the channels of invisible grace." Scripture, the early church, and the Anglican Church all taught this. "Here again," he writes, "I have not changed in opinion; I am as certain now on this point as I was in 1833, and have never ceased to be certain."[5]

On Newman's third proposition regarding the Church of Rome, however, things were quite different. At least since his conversion to Rome, of course, he had "utterly renounced and trampled upon" his early Tractarian view of the Roman Church as Antichrist. But, in 1833, although his feelings about the Roman Church had been softened through the influence of Froude and his experience in Italy, Newman felt it his duty, as a matter of "simple conscience" as an Anglican, to "protest against the Church of Rome." It was also necessary to protect himself against the charge of popery.[6]

As he looked back from a vantage point of three decades, this was Newman's presentation of the foundation the Movement elaborated and built on as it went forward: dogma, sacraments, and anti-Romanism. In sum, he writes: "Such was the position, such the defense, such the tactics, by which I thought that it was both incumbent on us, and possible for us, to meet that onset of Liberal principles, of which we were all in immediate anticipation, whether in the Church or in the University."[7]

The university was, in fact, the target of one of the early attacks. In March 1834 Newman took up his pen to defend against a bill which would admit Dissenters by dropping Oxford's matriculation requirement of subscribing to the Thirty-nine Articles. Cambridge required subscription only for the granting of a degree. But Newman found even that model unacceptable as a compromise. His pastoral view of university education, which had ended his tutorial career at Oriel, had no room for non-Anglicans whose lax principles might contaminate the faith of Anglican students and even tutors. He was able to rouse the university to a strongly hostile response, and win an easy victory.

The university, however, was not unanimously with Newman on this issue. A key opponent was R. D. Hampden, who, in 1832, had been appointed to one of the Oriel tutorial positions vacated by Newman and his friends, and, in early 1834, had been elected over Newman to the university chair in moral philosophy. Hampden had signed a petition against subscription reform. But later in 1834 he published a pamphlet titled *Observations on Religious Dissent, with particular reference to the use of religious tests in the university.* He sent a copy to Newman, who saw it as a Liberal attack on doctrine as mere theological opinion. Newman acknowledged its receipt by expressing his regret that it had been published, in that its principles tend to "make a shipwreck of Christian faith."[8] The following year, Hampden took exception to Newman's editing a collection of pamphlets on subscription, and particularly those attacking his view of it, as the work of a "fanatical persecuting spirit."[9] All this came to a climax early in 1836, when the Prime Minister, Lord Melbourne, appointed Hampden as Regius Professor of Divinity. Newman, of course, was furious. A protest to the king was organized. And Newman immediately produced a full-scale attack in an anonymous pamphlet, *Elucidations of Dr. Hampden's Theological Statements.* To an old friend, Newman wrote about Hampden: "There is no doctrine, however sacred, which he does not scoff at—and in his Moral Philosophy he adopts the lowest and most grovelling utilitarianism as the basis of Morals … ." He, "*judging by his writings*, is the most lucre loving, earthly minded, unlovely person one ever set eyes on."[10] But the appointment stood, and Newman and his friends had to be satisfied with a university Convocation vote expressing no confidence in Hampden on theology. Writing about this period in his *Apologia*, Newman says: "My great principle ever was, Live and let live."[11] Perhaps he had an opportunity to practice this principle later in 1836 when, taking his B. D. degree, Newman was required to declare the Thirty-nine Articles to the newly installed

Regius Professor of Divinity. The Hampden business had not been pretty, and, although Newman had scored some points, nasty terms of engagement had been established for future battles in which Newman and his Movement would be the target.

A YEAR OF LOSS

The year 1836 was an especially difficult one personally for Newman in many ways. On March 1st he learned of the death of Hurrell Froude, who for sometime had been living with his father in Devon. No loss could have been a more violent blow. Froude's health had been failing for years, and Newman, anticipating the imminent end, had written a week earlier that Froude's death would be "the greatest loss I could have. I shall be truly widowed … ." He felt that God, in taking his most intimate friend from him, was leading him "to depend on Him only." The loss was irreparable. To Newman, Froude was unearthly, angelic. He wrote of him to Bowden, his great undergraduate friend: "I never on the whole fell in with so gifted a person—in variety and perfection of gifts I think he far exceeded even Keble—for myself, I cannot describe what I owe to him as regards the intellectual principles of religion … ." Now the loneliness Newman had been suffering from Froude's absence from Oxford was permanent. He could only hope to be Froude's spiritual heir.[12]

Froude's death was a complete loss for Newman, but at least it had not been a matter of choice for Froude. In contrast, Newman had recently suffered losses of other close friends, which, while not complete, were indeed voluntary, the results of decisions to marry. And Newman found it difficult not to see these choices as betrayals—of a calling, and even of himself. Perhaps his most difficult loss to marriage was Keble, just the previous year while Newman was visiting Froude in Devon. The fact that Keble had married without telling anyone Newman took as an acknowledgement that "marriage is a very second rate business." It pained and sickened him.[13] Only a year earlier, when another close friend Henry Wilberforce had married, Newman had seen it as "nonsense—preparing marriage settlements and doing all he can to make himself one of the children of this world." This was the friend who Newman later claimed was the only one who had ever taken "that sort of affectionate interest in me … which a wife takes and none but she— and that interest, so be it, shall never be taken in me."[14] Newman had always been dependent on his friends' affection, and as he experienced the loss of some older ones he now turned to the support of younger ones like Frederic Rogers and Richard Church.[15]

This difficult year of 1836 also saw the death of Newman's mother in May, just a few weeks after his sister Jemima's marriage to John Mozley, and a few months before his sister Harriett's marriage to Thomas Mozley, John's younger brother and one of Newman's former Oriel students. Though deeply distressed by the loss of his mother, Newman was able to accept it as his mother's release from great suffering. Still, it reminded him of his regret that his work had kept him from spending more time with her and his sisters after they had moved closer to Oxford. They had been disappointed, and his feelings toward them had become very complicated. While he appreciated the wonderful service they gave to his Littlemore parish, they had not been in agreement with him on the Movement's principles, and this pained him greatly. They also disagreed with his severe attitude regarding his brothers' religious waywardness. In short, Newman was experiencing distance and loss in his family as well as with his friends, and all this was crystallized in the 1836 deaths of his mother and of his great friend Hurrell Froude.

THE MIDDLE WAY

From 1834 Newman had been at work on a presentation of his basic ecclesiological position. His old college friend John Bowden had alerted Newman to protect the Movement against the predictable accusation of popery. Newman's response was his famous *Via Media*, first in *Tracts*, then in lectures at St. Mary's and an exchange of published letters with a French priest, then in conversational form in *Home Thoughts Abroad*, and most fully in *Lectures on the Prophetical Office of the Church*, published in early 1837. His strategy was to disassociate the Church of England from the Reformers on one side and from Rome on the other, to define for it a middle way of its own, and in the process produce a positive system of Anglican theology based on the authority and rich but disparate theological work of his church's great Caroline Divines. Its foundation, of course, would be "dogma, the sacramental system, and anti-Romanism."[16]

While Protestants rely on private judgment of Scripture alone as their standard, Anglo-Catholics like Roman Catholics recognize Tradition as well as Scripture. Indeed, it is through Tradition, in Newman's view, that Christians receive both Scripture and the teaching of divine inspiration. Although Anglo-Catholics think the creed can be proven from Scripture, they in fact rely on Tradition's elucidation of the Bible as a source for Christian education. In this they are like Roman Catholics but different from Protestants, who avoid such external assistance in their interpretation of Scripture. Where Anglo-Catholics differ from the Romans is on the question of authority: the former opting for Antiquity, the latter for the infallible church itself. For Newman the test of true Tradition is "Catholicity, Antiquity, and consent of Fathers," and one's judgment on it, as on life's other great questions, is a matter of probability.[17] And if patristic teaching seems too imprecise and unsystematic to be a practical guide, Anglo-Catholics have the Creeds and the Prayer Book to follow. By distinguishing between Episcopal Tradition (the apostolic deposit of faith) and Prophetic Tradition (the ongoing, living interpretation of Revelation), Newman explains how the Anglicans and Romans can be united on the former while divided on the latter.[18]

The Lectures on the Prophetical Office were hardly off the press when Newman began an expansion of his "middle way" to the question of justification. The spring of 1837 saw a set of lectures on the topic at St. Mary's. Much hard work and anxiety followed through the year, and by early 1838 the volume of Lectures on Justification appeared. Again, the attempt is to navigate a safe and true course between the mistaken and dangerous extremes of Rome and the Reformers. Rome stressed salvation through renewal, obedience, and good works; the Reformers through faith alone. Newman's strategy was to move below the surface and find in grace the single, common principle of both. For him, justi-fication is brought about "by the power of the Spirit, or rather by His presence within us," and "faith and renewal are both present also, but as fruits" of that divine indwelling.[19]

In the course of his discussion of justification, Newman points out that Luther responds to the Catholic teaching that love is the true form of justifying faith by arguing that it "makes our thoughts centre on ourselves," whereas the doctrine of faith "secure[s] us against self-contemplation." This is an especially interesting point inasmuch as a tendency toward "contemplating ourselves instead of Christ" was one of Newman's complaints about Evangelicals.[20]

FROUDE'S REMAINS

After a long illness (the reason for their Mediterranean trip together in 1833) Newman's great friend Hurrell Froude had died, as noted above, in early 1836. Froude had been a powerful influence on him, and Newman, who could not imagine a greater loss, felt "truly widowed."[21] Froude's papers had been entrusted by his father, the archdeacon, to Newman and Keble for possible publication. After some consultation with Keble and other colleagues, Newman set about editing them with definite enthusiasm. But by the end of 1837, when the first two volumes were ready for publication, Newman's attitude had shifted from enthusiasm to anxiety. Newman realized that Froude's very private papers had something to irritate, aggravate, even scandalize people on all sides; though severe on Rome, the papers were strongly Catholic and anti-Protestant, and they contained detailed accounts of such private aspects of Froude's life as temptations and fastings. Despite Newman's explanatory introduction, the reactions to Froude's *Remains*, from friends and foes alike, fulfilled his worst fears, and did as much to focus negative attention on the Movement as anything Newman and other Tract authors had published.

Prominent in the barrage of protests against Froude's *Remains* was a university sermon preached in May 1838 by Godfrey Faussett, Lady Margaret Professor of Divinity: "Revival of Popery." Though aimed at the *Remains*, Faussett's critique was more widely directed against the entire Tractarian program, and Newman took up his pen in reply immediately upon the sermon's publication in June: *A Letter to the Rev. Godfrey Faussett, D.D.* To Faussett's basic charge that Froude's ideas amounted to an attempt to revive popery in the Anglican Church, Newman responded that these ideas had been held and taught by such Anglican Divines as Hooker, Andrewes, Laud and many others, and argued in detail on issues ranging from the Real Presence and the Sacrifice of the Mass to Monasteries and the Pope.

Though Newman's influence was at its height at this point, his feelings were not immune to criticism, especially when it came from his bishop, as it did in the summer of 1838. Prodded by Newman's opponents, Bishop Bagot of Oxford used the occasion of his Triennial Charge to mildly caution that certain unspecified Tractarian points might be misunderstood by some readers and thus harmful. Though couched within general praise for the Movement, this warning hurt

Newman, who had great respect for episcopal authority, and he offered to withdraw the *Tracts*. The bishop made it clear that withdrawal was unnecessary, and when his Charge was published he added a note denying any intention of censuring the *Tracts*. Despite this minor victory for Newman, the episode highlighted just how vulnerable the Movement was even as it achieved its greatest strength. Success invited attack.

At the beginning of 1838, with the *British Critic* in desperate need of an editor, Newman had reluctantly agreed to accept the position in order to guarantee its Catholicity. Among his own writings for the journal was an April 1839 article titled "The State of Religious Parties." Newman did not realize it at the time, but, as he later recalled in his *Apologia*, this article, appearing at the height of his Anglican influence, contained "the last words which I ever spoke as an Anglican to Anglicans."[22] In it Newman identifies the three main parties in the Church of England: Liberalism, Evangelicalism, and Anglo-Catholicism. He had a personal knowledge of all three. Liberalism, with which he had flirted in his mid-twenties, was "too cold" to be popular. Evangelicalism, the religion of his adolescent conversion and early twenties, was the largest party, but, lacking an "internal principle of union, permanence, and consistency," was not real, not living, and thus destined for ruin.[23] Newman had rejected both long ago. Anglo-Catholicism, in contrast, was not only real and living, but responded intellectually to the spiritual awakening manifested by the popular success of Romantic authors like Walter Scott. With the "spirit of Luther ... dead," Anglo-Catholicism was, in Newman's judgment, also the one Anglican party with the spiritual and intellectual strength necessary to confront threats lying beyond the Church of England. Between the extreme alternatives of Roman Catholicism and Rationalistic unbelief, Newman saw Anglo-Catholicism as the "true and intelligible mean," the *Via Media* delineated by the seventeenth-century Divines.[24] "The current of the age cannot be stopped," he claimed, "but it may be directed; and it is better that it should find its way into the Anglican port, than that it should be propelled into Popery, or drifted upon unbelief."[25] For Newman, of course, the serious challenger was Roman Catholicism. And, as he later recounted this period in his *Apologia*, the battle lines were drawn between "the Anglican *Via Media* and the popular religion of Rome," the first standing on Apostolicity, the second on Catholicity.[26] That, at least, was Newman's view in early 1839. But things were soon to change.

IN A MIRROR CLEARLY

In his *Apologia* Newman relates that during the summer of 1839, while studying the history of the Monophysites, he received a "shock which was to cast out of [his] imagination all middle courses and compromises for ever." He explains this shock in terms of discovering himself on the heretical side of a structural analogy: "My stronghold was Antiquity; now here, in the middle of the fifth century, I found ... Christendom of the sixteenth and the nineteenth centuries reflected. I saw my face in that mirror, and I was a Monophysite. The Church of the *Via Media* was in the position of the Oriental communion, Rome was where she now is; and the Protestants were the Eutychians." This was his first doubt about the "tenableness of Anglicanism."[27]

About two months later Newman was shocked again, this time by a line from Augustine quoted in an article by Nicholas Wiseman on the Donatists: "Securus judicat orbis terrarum." He understood these words to mean that "the deliberate judgment, in which the whole Church at length rests and acquiesces, is an infallible prescription and a final sentence against such portions of it as protest and secede." Here in Augustine "Antiquity was deciding against itself," and for Newman "the theory of the *Via Media* was absolutely pulverized."[28]

Reflecting back on this experience more than two decades later, Newman thought that for years before it he "must have had something of an habitual notion, though it was latent, and had never led [him] to distrust [his] own convictions, that [his] mind had not found its own ultimate rest, and that in some sense or other [he] was on a journey." In any case, the experience was a "dreadful misgiving" which caused him "dismay and disgust." Still, he "became excited at the view thus opened," though before long "the vivid impression upon [his] imagination faded away." In the *Apologia* he sums up the experience this way: "The heavens had opened and closed again. The thought for the moment had been, 'The Church of Rome will be found right after all;' and then it had vanished. My old convictions remained as before." But he "had seen the shadow of a hand upon the wall.... . He who has seen a ghost, cannot be as if he had never seen it."[29]

From this experience a single question emerged for Newman: "The one question was, what was I to do? I had to make up my mind for myself, and others could not help me. I determined to be guided, not by my imagination, but by my reason." On the other hand, he felt a positive doubt: "whether the suggestion did not come from below. Then I said to myself, Time alone can solve that question.... If it came from above, it would come again ... and with more definite outlines and greater cogency and consistency of proof." Meanwhile, with the *Via Media* shattered, he felt that he was nearly a pure Protestant with no positive theology, and that he had only his three original principles to fall back on: dogma, sacrament, and anti-Romanism. He saw the first two as stronger in Rome, but the third was still a stumbling block: though his reason was now convinced otherwise, his adolescent prejudice of Rome as Antichrist was still a "stain upon [his] imagination." And he did have strong objections to Rome's abuses and excesses, as well as to its secular and political conduct, even though he was beginning to sense that he had uncritically allowed himself to be influenced by the Anglican Divines, taking for granted what they said about Rome.[30] Beyond his own situation, Newman was also concerned about the Movement: about defections to Rome (especially among the younger members) and about schism within the Anglican Church. He attempted to address these problems in a January 1840 *British Critic* article in which, using the model of Israel remaining a holy people even after the destruction of the Temple, he argued for the "Catholicity of the Anglican Church," despite the church's fragmentation. But he was also concerned about a broader crisis in religion, and wondered if any church other than the Roman could stand against the Liberal attack.[31]

For Lent 1840 Newman decided to move out to Littlemore, where he got enthusiastically engaged in parish work, especially at the school. While there, he also bought several acres near the church, with the thought of starting a monastic community. During the summer Newman found himself advising friends who were contemplating a move to Rome. Although he felt difficulties of his own, he told them he was convinced that he should stay put, and advised them to do likewise. He saw individual moves as following "private judgment," which required "overpowering evidence" that going over was God's will, that it was thus an absolute duty.[32] For himself, Newman at this point did not feel that duty. He did feel enough suspicion about his position in the Anglican Church, however, to ask Keble's advice about giving up St. Mary's. He was concerned that his preaching might be pushing some individuals toward Rome. Keble thought he should stay at St.

Mary's, that leaving could cause scandal, while staying would allow him to be a stabilizing factor. Newman was convinced, and stayed. He wrote to Rogers that "a good conscience is all that one wants."[33]

In the first months of 1841 Newman felt it necessary to respond to two Liberal statements: Henry Hart Milman's *History of Christianity* and Sir Robert Peel's speech at the new Tamworth Reading Room. Both responses reasserted Newman's fundamental distinction between two worlds: the visible world is the "instrument, yet veil" of the "truer and higher" invisible world.[34] For Newman, Milman focuses too narrowly on the visible side of Christianity, while Peel's understanding of knowledge and education is too shallow, without recognition that "apprehension of the unseen is the only known principle capable of subduing moral evil, educating the multitude, and organizing society . . . ."[35]

But the publication event of early 1841 was the "anonymous" *Tract 90*, which appeared the week after Newman's fortieth birthday on February 21st. Newman's practical aim, he tells us in the *Apologia*, was to calm the restless members of the Movement who were happy with neither his *Via Media* nor his argument against Rome. To keep them from "Rome or schism or an uncomfortable conscience,"[36] he needed to show that the Anglican Church, especially in its Thirty-nine Articles, was in a true sense one with the Catholic Church of Athanasius and Augustine. He viewed the attempt as an *"experimentum crucis."*[37] His claim is that the Articles, "the offspring of an uncatholic age, are, through God's good providence, to say the least, not uncatholic, and may be subscribed by those who aim at being catholic in heart and doctrine." The conclusion to his detailed argument is that "it is a *duty* which we owe both to the Catholic Church and to our own, to take our reformed confessions in the most Catholic sense they will admit; we have no duties towards their framers."[38] The norm for interpretation, in short, is the Catholic sense, not the mind of the framers.

The reaction was immediate. Within two weeks the university Vice-Chancellor and the Heads of Houses issued a public censure. Within another two weeks, after some negotiations, Newman was required to write a public letter to his bishop acknowledging the bishop's judgment that *Tract 90* was "objectionable" and that the *Tracts* should be "discontinued."[39] But that appeared to end the matter. Newman could take satisfaction that nothing had been suppressed, nothing condemned.

The question of "Private Judgment" was, as already noted, clearly a central and difficult issue for Newman and his colleagues, and he now devoted an entire article to it for the *British Critic*. He does not mince words: "when Private Judgment moves in the direction of innovation, it may well be regarded at first with suspicion and treated with severity." Foreshadowing the coming years, he continues: "if any men have strong feelings, they should pay for them; if they think it a duty to unsettle things established, they should show their earnestness by being willing to suffer ... ." Private judgment, he says, "if not a duty, is a sin." Of course his context here is religious change, and it will perhaps surprise some to find the man who would a few years later write that "to live is to change, and to be perfect is to have changed often," claiming that "serious religious changes have a *prima facie* case against them ... ." Change, he asserts, "is really the characteristic of error, and unalterableness the attribute of truth, of holiness, of Almighty God Himself ... ."[40] Change, in a word, must be justified. Again foreshadowing things to come, Newman holds that private judgment should not be about doctrines, but about teachers. Which body is the true teaching church?

These reflections on private judgment would soon become even more intimately personal for Newman. For as they were appearing in the July *British Critic*, his situation was beginning to become much more difficult. As he would later relate in the *Apologia*, between July and November 1841 he received the now famous "three blows" which broke him.

THREE BLOWS

Newman was in Littlemore quietly working on a translation of St. Athanasius when his "trouble returned ... . The ghost had come a second time." He found clearly in the Arians an even bolder version of what he had earlier discovered in the Monophysites: that "the pure Arians were the Protestants, the semi-Arians were the Anglicans, and that Rome now was what it was then. The truth lay, not with the *Via Media*, but with what was called 'the extreme party'"—with Rome.[41]

The second blow was political. Newman now realized he had been wrong in thinking he had emerged from the *Tract 90* business in relatively good shape. It was not over. Bishops now individually began condemning the *Tract* in what would become over the next three years a long series of hostile charges. Though the *Tract* was not silenced—something individual bishops could not do out of synod— Newman saw the charges as a serious sign that the day might be coming when it would be his duty to leave the Anglican Church should it repudiate the Catholic in favor of the Protestant. Whether his church was Catholic or heretic was now a live question. And the next episode did not encourage him.

The third blow, which "finally shattered" Newman's faith in the Church of England, was the installation of an Anglican bishop in Jerusalem. The problem, as Newman saw it, was that the new bishopric, a joint venture with Protestant Prussia, would bring together Protestants, Jews, Druses, and Monophysites under Anglican auspices, for the purpose of projecting British influence into the Middle East. Regarding this as exactly the kind of Protestantizing he feared, on November 11th he sent a formal protest to the Archbishop of Canterbury. Looking back in his *Apologia*, he viewed the whole affair as "one of the greatest mercies. It brought me," he wrote, "on to the beginning of the end."[42] Still, at the time it was only a beginning, an intellectual beginning. He felt no call to *do* anything, no call to go to Rome. As he counseled others, he felt that he too had a duty to stay until he had a duty to go. That would take some time.

Newman was now between the proverbial rock and a hard place. He could no longer hold the old Anglican principles, but neither could he move toward corrupt Rome. Ever since his Monophysite discovery in 1839, he had realized that the *Via Media* was an "impossible idea." He had then turned to the note of Sanctity or Holiness as the true test of a church. "According to this theory," he explained in the *Apologia*, "a religious body is part of the One Catholic and Apostolic Church, if it has the succession and the creed of the Apostles, with the note of holiness of life … ." But now he had seen the bishops and people of his church reject primitive Catholic doctrine, and attempt to rid the church of those who held it. So he had lost that toehold, and had to reach for another.[43]

In December 1841 Newman set out his new position in four sermons at St. Mary's. He capsulized the view's main spiritual point in a letter to an "intimate friend." After acknowledging the powerful feelings that can attract one to Rome, but clearly stating his duty to remain an Anglican, he explains that he has "a much more definite view of the (promised) inward evidence of the Presence of Christ with us in the Sacraments, now that the outward notes of it are being removed."

And he adds a reference to the analogy with Judaism made in his sermons: "I am content to be with Moses in the desert, or with Elijah excommunicated from the Temple."[44] This move from external notes and objective theory to internal notes and subjective view stunned Newman's moderate Tractarian friends. As he put it in the *Apologia*, they were "surprised and offended at a line of argument, novel, and, as it appeared to them, wanton, which threw the whole controversy into confusion, stultified my former principles, and substituted, as they would consider, a sort of methodistic self-contemplation, especially abhorrent both to my nature and to my past professions, for the plain and honest tokens, as they were commonly received, of a divine mission in the Anglican Church."[45] These friends saw Newman foundering. Having lost one certainty, he was struggling for his spiritual life. What turned out to be a transitional phase could at the time only have been experienced as a desperate nightmare.

LITTLEMORE

A planned 1842 move to permanent residence in Littlemore would take Newman away from the external battle (though not from prying newspaper inquiry), but would offer no safe haven from internal turmoil. He had not felt comfortable in Oxford, and facilities in Littlemore would allow for monastic-like companionship with those of similar sympathies, especially with younger men in the Movement. In fact, younger members, who knew more of Rome than of the *Via Media*, were beginning to dominate the Movement, and, given Newman's difficulties with many original members, inevitably exerted an influence on him, despite significant differences in opinion or "cast of mind."[46] By the end of 1842 Newman was in correspondence with the Roman Catholic Charles Russell, and had written a retraction of his anti-Roman statements, explaining that over the years he had been repeating the views of Anglican Divines, with the hope of staving off charges of Romanism from his critics. Published anonymously early in 1843, this retraction helped to ease his guilty sense that he had been misleading people who trusted him about his true (positive) feelings toward Rome.[47] During January he was also writing a sermon on doctrinal development that he preached early in February and then published the same month in a volume with other of his *University Sermons*, an early pre-Tractarian group and a more recent set focused on faith and reason. This last of the sermons presented the core of his argument on development, which he would expand over the next two years. That the first printing sold out in two weeks gives some indication of the growing interest in Newman and his position.

Preaching at St. Mary's may have only intensified the interior conflict Newman was experiencing between holding the pulpit at St. Mary's and feeling closer and closer to Rome. In a letter seeking advice from his trusted friend Keble, he shocks even himself in writing: "I consider the Roman Catholic Communion the Church of the Apostles."[48] As the months of 1843 passed by, he felt less and less comfortable at St. Mary's, and Keble's objections to his retirement lessened. In June the university suspended Pusey from preaching, its first formal act against the Movement. Then, at the end of the summer, Newman was stunned to learn that one of the Littlemore group was about to make the move to Rome. That decision was the push Newman needed, and on September 7th, seeing his position as untenable, he gave up St. Mary's. At the end of the month he preached his last Anglican sermon at Littlemore: "The Parting of Friends." In his *Apologia* Newman quotes from a letter he wrote to his friend Henry Manning on October 25th: "I must tell you then frankly ... that it is from no disappointment, irritation, or impatience, that I have, whether rightly or wrongly, resigned St. Mary's—but because I think the Church of Rome the Catholic Church, and ours not a part of the Catholic Church, because not in communion with Rome, and I feel that I could not honestly be a teacher in it any longer."[49]

Through 1844 Newman only fell into deeper confusion. His anguish is manifested in letters to confidants, including Bowden, Keble, Pusey, Wilberforce, and especially Mrs. William Froude. In February he told Pusey that, though he felt no present call to action, he had an on again, off again, but growing conviction that Anglicans were not part of the Catholic Church. He dreaded the day this conviction might reach "full persuasion." Meanwhile, he hoped for some external sign, and consoled himself with the belief that, as he had recently told Mrs. Froude, "Time alone can turn a view into a conviction." He realized that people act on convictions, not simply ideas; that imagination and feeling do not quickly turn into convictions; that development in conviction and action takes time. He wanted his present view kept secret among his closest friends, but gave them permission to share with others the impact the events of 1839 had had on his view of Rome. He felt that his move to Rome was inevitable, but he did not yet have the call. He was afraid of being misled by his feelings, of being under a delusion. He wanted to act only from duty. He recognized that Rome was the true church; but his feelings and imagination did not support a move. The concrete sense of what a move would sacrifice, and the pain of anticipated loss were far more powerful than the attraction of a church he did not really know, with which he had no tangible connection. He realized the difficulty and high price of serious change. In the *Apologia* he relates how, at the end of 1844, he "came to the resolution of writing an *Essay on Doctrinal Development*; and then, if, at the end of it, [his] convictions in favour of the Roman Church were not weaker, of taking the necessary steps for admission into her fold."[50] It is not clear how he expected such an intellectual effort to settle the issue for him.

THE HOME STRETCH

Publicly, things got off to a bad start in 1845. The previous year the Tractarian W. G. Ward had published his *Ideal of a Christian Church*, claiming that only Rome could meet the book's test. He also claimed that as an Anglican and Balliol Fellow he could maintain Roman doctrine. The College Heads petitioned the University Convocation to condemn Ward's book and to revoke his degrees, which it did in February 1845. The Heads also used the occasion to propose a Convocation censure of *Tract 90*, but that move failed when Newman's friend R. W. Church, a proctor, exercised his veto power. Still, Newman thought the whole business might be the kind of external sign he had been hoping for.

Newman now felt his conviction for a move to Rome growing stronger, and he began telling family and friends that he might be leaving the Anglican Church by Christmas. In March he wrote to his sister Jemima: "What means of judging can I have more than I have? What maturity of mind am I to expect? If I am right to move at all, surely it is high time not to delay about it longer." He rehearsed for her the loss, the risk, the sacrifice, the pain of such a move, a move that he thought made sense only because he was called to do it. He would be leaving everyone he loved, and going, he said, "to those whom I do not know and of whom I expect very little—I am making myself an outcast, and that at my age. Oh, what can it be but a stern necessity which causes this?" And he confided to Jemima, who was very distressed by the prospect of his move, that he had begun to fear the possibility of suddenly dying outside the Roman Church.[51]

By the summer of 1845 Newman's mind was pretty much set, and he could "almost think the crisis over." Indeed, he had reached a dichotomous clarity: he did "not see any medium between disowning Christianity, and taking the Church of Rome." "If Christianity is one and the same at all times," he wrote, "then I must believe, not what the Reformers have carved out of it, but what the Catholic Church holds." Despite his new clarity, he still agonized during these months as he wrote and re-wrote the book in which he was trying to explain the fact of developing doctrine in a Christianity that is "one and the same at all times."[52]

For Newman the question of doctrinal development is a matter of reconciling continuity and change: how throughout continuous change can there be continuing identity; how, specifically, with all its additions can the Roman Church be the church of the Apostles? Change in itself presented no problem for Newman. The adolescent Evangelical who had taken "Growth the only evidence of life" as a basic proverb now asserted that "to live is to change, and to be perfect is to have changed often." In fact, Newman, as we have seen, was very familiar with change in his own life. Indeed, in an important sense the *Essay* is implicitly also autobiographical, Newman's first *apologia*, a defense, an explanation to himself, to his friends, and ultimately to the world, of yet another major change in himself—the most public and difficult, even if not personally the most important, change in his life. These two dimensions, the explicit theological question and the implicit personal motivation, go hand in hand: to satisfactorily answer the first would be to successfully defend the second.

Newman's objective in the *Essay*, then, is to reconcile the fact of doctrinal change in the Roman Church with the enduring identity of the apostolic faith, and thus to justify his move to Rome. His strategy is to conceive Christian faith as a living idea which inevitably changes as it takes on the variety of challenges presented in its mental environment. Through such a process of encounter the faith is fulfilled as its many aspects are made explicit. But along with authentic developments of the ancient faith are also corruptions. And to distinguish the one from the other, Newman specified seven "tests" (characteristics) of authentic development. In summary, a development is healthy "if it retains one and the same type, the same principles, the same organization; if its beginnings anticipate its subsequent phases, and its later phenomena protect and subserve its earlier; if it has a power of assimilation and revival, and a vigorous action from first to last."[53] At the bottom line, Newman's detailed examination of Roman doctrinal changes finds that they meet the tests, and thus the way is clear for him to make the move.

In his *Apologia* Newman explains the *Essay's* effect on him: "As I advanced, my difficulties so cleared away that I ceased to speak of 'the Roman Catholics,' and boldly called them Catholics. Before I got to the end, I resolved to be received, and the book remains in the state in which it was then, unfinished."[54] In the *Essay's* Advertisement, he wrote that, while the book was in a drawn out printing process, "he recognized in himself a conviction of the truth of the conclusion to which the discussion leads, so clear as to supersede further deliberation."[55] Thus, on October 3rd he wrote succinctly to Hawkins, the Oriel provost: "I shall be obliged to you if you will remove my name from the books of the College and the University."[56] And on October 9th at Littlemore he was received into the Roman Catholic Church by Father Dominic Barberi, an Italian Passionist who had recently received Newman's Littlemore companion J. D. Dalgairns. At the end of a long journey the agony was finally over: "it was like coming into port after a rough sea ... ."[57] The image of a rough sea reminds us that 1845 was also the year Newman's countryman Sir John Franklin had set out on his ill-fated Arctic expedition in search of a Northwest Passage to the Pacific. Spiritually, Newman's exploration had been equally perilous, but ultimately successful in his discovery of a personal Southeast Passage to Rome.

2. REVIEWING THE JOURNEY OF ECCLESIAL CONVERSION

Conversion, as we have seen in earlier chapters, is an about-face, a significant change of direction, a fundamental horizon shift *from* one reality *to* another, indeed, from one *world* to another. It often involves two distinct moments: a negative deconversion *from* and a positive conversion *to*.[58] Newman's letter to the Oriel provost asking that his name be removed from the books represented his negative moment of *deconversion* from the Anglican Church. His positive moment of *con-*

version was signified by his reception into the Roman Catholic Church at the hand of Father Barberi.

Newman clearly experienced significant development during the dozen years of the Oxford Movement. Every dimension of his being—from affective and cognitive to moral and religious—underwent profound change. The main focus of my remarks here, however, will be on the cognitive and the moral. The central point I will develop is that between 1839 and 1841 Newman experienced a cognitive conversion of content in his understanding of the church, and that this cognitive conversion, when turned directly on himself by 1843, demanded an enormously difficult moral decision which Newman made only in 1845: his ecclesial conversion, his going over from Oxford to Rome.

Newman's 1845 move to Rome has been the object of endless interpretations, including his own defensive presentation in the *Apologia* and most recently Frank Turner's controversial revisionist version.[59] Here I will bring together the strengths of each of these two views— Newman's insistence on the intellectual, spiritual conversion *to* Roman Catholicism and Turner's focus on the affective, social deconversion *from* Oxonian Anglicanism—into a new constructive synthesis. This new synthesis, moreover, will itself be situated within an original overarching interpretation of Newman's ecclesial shift, a three-phase process emphasizing *cognitive* conversion and moral *decision*. We will see, indeed, that because Turner actually explores Newman's deconversion from the Anglican Church rather than his conversion to the Roman Church, he in fact helpfully highlights the existential deconversion factors that made Newman's transitional process so long and difficult.

Before considering Newman's cognitive conversion of 1839-1841, his personal appropriation of it by 1843, and his crucial decision of 1845, though, we must examine his intellectual horizon of the late 1830s and early 1840s in which these events occurred. We will begin this examination by the indirect route of focusing on Newman's understanding of his intellectual enemies in this period, an issue of some controversy.

LIBERALS AND EVANGELICALS

At many points throughout his *Apologia* Newman claims that his intellectual enemy during the 1830s and 1840s was Liberalism.[60] Indeed, in the second edition he even includes a long Note explaining this "system of opinion."[61] Recently, Frank Turner has taken major exception to this claim. Turner argues that Evangelicalism, not Liberalism, was the primary enemy targeted by Newman and other Tractarians. The meaning of Liberalism, he says, had changed significantly between the 1830s and the 1860s, and in his 1864 *Apologia* Newman exploited that difference by tagging his 1830s religious enemies—"evangelical Dissenters, churchmen willing to accommodate modestly their grievances, moderate Protestants, and establishment evangelicals"—with the label Liberal, which by the 1860s referred to secularism, something all Christians, Protestants as well as Roman Catholics, opposed. "Evangelical Protestantism," Turner claims, "and not political or secular liberalism in and of itself had been the Tractarian enemy. It was this assault against evangelical Protestantism lying at the heart of the Tractarian Movement that ... Newman omitted and concealed in the *Apologia*, where he wrote as a controversialist seeking to reshape and rescue his personal public reputation." As a result, in Turner's view, "the Tractarian Movement of the 1830s and 1840s, as constituting the most extensive, vigorous theological and intellectual assault of the century on evangelical Protestantism, became lost to memory or became transformed, and thus tamed, into a struggle for a universal Catholic truth in the face of an opposing liberal religion."[62]

My purpose here is not to decide this issue in favor of either Newman or Turner. Rather, leaving Turner's interpretation of Newman's motives aside, I intend to offer a reconciling view, to suggest an approach that can subsume the substance of both claims. I will propose that Newman opposed both Liberalism and Evangelicalism, and that he attacked these two enemies for the same reason: he regarded them, at bottom, as two versions of his one great enemy—subjectivism.

We noted above, near the end of chapter 2, that during his late twenties Newman came to appreciate objectivity in a particularly strong way as a result of his significant cognitive conversion at that time. We also noted early in this present chapter that Newman from his first conversion at age fifteen had regarded dogma as his fundamental principle in religion. This principle was only sharpened, of course, by the heightened sense of objectivity issuing from his later cognitive conversion. Put simply, the objectivity of dogma was Newman's top religious priority as the Tractarian Movement got underway. It is not surprising, then, that he identified subjectivism, the very antithesis and subversion of objectively true doctrine, as the primary enemy.

We have seen that Newman was intimately familiar with the two major forms subjectivism took in his day: Evangelicalism and Liberalism. His first conversion at age fifteen was clearly a conversion to an Evangelical form of Christianity. And when he moved away from Evangelicalism in his twenties, he moved toward the Liberalism of the Oriel Noetics, his common room colleagues at Oxford. Evangelicalism was an *emotional* version of subjectivism; Liberalism was a *rationalistic* version. But, as different as they were, both were at root identical in their subjectivist denial of the objective truth of Newman's cherished dogma. Both were essentially different forms of egocentrism. Newman had been heavily influenced by significant individuals drawing him toward these positions, by Walter Mayers in the case of Evangelicalism, and by Whately and Hawkins in the case of Liberalism. But, thanks perhaps to his basic dogmatic instinct, he probably never gave himself fully to either position. It was finally under the influence of Pusey, Froude, and Keble that Newman experienced the cognitive conversion of his late twenties, which allowed him to grasp clearly the truth of his objective principle of dogma, and to recognize the error in the subjectivism of both Evangelicalism and Liberalism. Indeed, in writing about Rationalism, Newman linked it with Evangelicalism. In the spirit of the modern age, he charges, "The Rationalist makes himself his own centre, not his Maker." And for this Newman blames Evangelicalism, which attends "to the heart itself, not to anything external to us, whether creed, actions, or rituals." It "is really a specious form of trusting man rather than God," and is therefore "in its nature Rationalistic."[63]

Rationalism, as understood by Newman, undermines objective truth. "By Objective Truth," he says, "is meant the Religious System considered as existing in itself, external to this or that particular mind." In contrast to this notion of objective truth, which some might consider objectivism, there is subjective truth. "By Subjective," he continues, "is meant that which each mind receives in particular, and considers to be such. To believe in Objective truth is to throw ourselves forward upon that which we have but partially mastered or made subjective; to embrace, maintain, and use general propositions which are larger than our own capacity, … as if we were contemplating what is real and independent of human judgment."[64] Whereas Newman identifies faith with objective truth, Rationalism restricts it to subjective experience. Private judgment, of course, is the most explicit claim to subjective truth, and thus, in Newman's mind, extends the fundamental error of subjectivism to the whole of Protestantism. In a late 1840 letter to Keble, he asserts that "Rationalism is the great evil of the day.... I am more certain that the Protestant [spirit], which I oppose, leads to infidelity, than that which I recommend [i.e., the Catholic spirit], leads to Rome."[65] In an 1841 letter to a "zealous Catholic layman," Newman links Protestantism with Liberalism, "the characteristic of the destined Antichrist": "The spirit of lawlessness came in with the Reformation, and Liberalism is its offspring."[66]

So, whether inside the church earlier or outside the church later, for Newman the great enemy of the objective truth of doctrine was subjectivism, be it under the name of Rationalism, Evangelicalism, or Liberalism. Whatever reason Newman had for identifying the enemy as Liberalism in his 1864 *Apologia*, and whatever advantages he might have gained by that identification, he was in fact writing about the same great enemy he had detected in Evangelicalism and called Rationalism in the 1830s, and that enemy was subjectivism, the egocentric denial of the objective truth of Catholic doctrines. In the 1830s, of course, Newman held those Catholic doctrines as an Anglican, and we have seen how he argued for a *Via Media* between Protestantism and Roman Catholicism to justify his position. However, when his *Via Media* began to crumble in 1839, Newman faced a new problem, which was greater and even more personal than anything he had dealt with before. But, before turning to that story, we must consider a central intellectual issue Newman engaged in his pre-conversion years: the relationship between faith and reason.

FAITH AND REASON

Early in 1839, before the summer of his Monophysite ghost, Newman began a series of university sermons on faith and reason. Convinced that many controversies stemmed from lack of clear definitions, he set out to provide some clarity on the standard Christian and Catholic meanings of the words faith and reason. What he accomplished, however, is a quite distinctive understanding of these terms and their relationship. Whereas most writers of the time set faith and reason off against each other as very different realities, Newman's special contribution was to expand the commonly accepted Enlightenment meaning of reason in a way that allowed him to relate it positively to faith. Indeed, Newman himself had some years earlier quite explicitly used what he called a "narrower signification" of reason and opposed it to faith in a sermon tellingly titled "The Usurpations of Reason" (1831). There reason was regarded as an "instrument at best, in the hands of the legitimate judge, spiritual discernment." In this early sermon Newman realized that reason in its largest sense "stands for all in which man differs from the brutes, and so includes in its signification the faculty of distinguishing between right and wrong, and the directing principle in conduct." But then his point was to argue against the narrow secular and rationalistic meaning of the term, and its erroneous intrusion into the realm of the moral and religious. Thus, perhaps in reaction to his own recent dalliance with rationalistic Liberalism, this 1831 sermon was framed as an argument against reason in this narrow sense and for faith as an almost moral, practical principle.[67]

By 1839, however, Newman was developing a quite different approach to the faith and reason relationship. He begins by contrasting the two. As commonly understood by Christian writers, faith is not against reason, but it does not depend on reason. Reason demands evidence, "direct and definite proof"; faith, by contrast, proceeds more on "antecedent considerations" such as "previously entertained principles, views, and wishes," or, in Newman's classic phrase, on "antecedent probabilities." These probabilities are connected with character: "A good man and a bad man will think very different things probable." So, insofar as we are responsible for our character, we are also responsible for our faith. Though faith does not depend on reason, it is not entirely independent of proof. But, Newman asserts, "proof need not be the subject of analysis, or take a methodical form, or be complete and symmetrical, in the believing mind ... ." Probability, he says, is its life. For Newman, "it is antecedent probability that gives meaning to those arguments from facts which are commonly called the Evidence of Revelation; ... probability is to fact, as the soul is to the body ... ."[68]

Having contrasted faith with reason, Newman turns to a positive definition: faith is "the reasoning of a religious mind," of "a right or renewed heart, which acts upon presumptions rather than evidence; which speculates and ventures on the future when it cannot make sure of it." Faith is an "exercise of Reason." Reason proceeds from things perceived to things unperceived on the basis of assumption. Even in the best exercise of reason something is taken for granted; "there must be something assumed ultimately which is incapable of proof ... ." Thus faith is like other uses of reason, in which "we must assume something to prove anything, and can gain nothing without a venture." Faith, as stated above, is linked to character, to the "moral state of the agent." For Newman, the bottom line on faith is: "We *believe*, because we *love*." Thus he capsulizes his position on faith in moral terms. "Right Faith is the faith of a right mind. Faith is an intellectual act; right Faith is an intellectual act, done in a certain moral disposition. Faith is an act of Reason, viz. a reasoning upon presumptions; right Faith is a reasoning upon holy, devout, and enlightened presumptions."[69]

To say that faith is an act of reason is not to claim that its reasoning is always analytic or reflective. Using the analogy of mountain climbing, Newman explains that reasoning is "a living spontaneous energy within us," that we commonly reason "not by rule, but by an inward faculty." Only occasionally is this informal reasoning analyzed formally. Newman makes this distinction succinctly: "all men have a reason, but not all men can give a reason." He continues: "We may denote, then, these two exercises of mind as reasoning and arguing, or as conscious and unconscious reasoning, or as Implicit Reason and Explicit Reason." This enlarged sense of reason allowed Newman to understand faith and reason, finally, not negatively as opposed to each other, but positively in terms of each other. Faith is an act of implicit reason based on antecedent probabilities rooted in character, a character formed, in Newman's mind, by supernatural grace.[70]

Still, though faith is usually an act of implicit reason, when faith is challenged, as Newman's was after his ghostly summer of 1839, one turns reflexively to the analytic exercise of explicit reason in order to examine one's grounds. This is what Newman did and what he meant by being determined to be guided by reason rather than by imagination or by feeling.[71]

REASON AND AFFECTIVE IMAGINATION

With the Monophysite ghost and the Augustinian echo in the summer of 1839 Newman began a new stage of his life's journey, a cognitive conversion of content regarding the identity of the Catholic Church. This cognitive conversion constituted a key dimension of the multi-year process that culminated with Newman moving in 1845 from the Anglican Church to the Roman Church, the move commonly called his "conversion." As important as this cognitive conversion was for Newman, it was only one part of a long and grueling process. For beyond (1) grasping a *new view* of the true church in the abstract, Newman had to (2) make an existential application of this new view *to himself*, and then (3) *decide to act* on this new ecclesial self-understanding. These necessary antecedents to the move to Rome would take time and much anguish.

Newman certainly had a sharp appreciation of the importance of the imagination, as we noted above, for example, in his assessment of the long-lived anti-papal stain on his imagination from his teen years when he was taught that the pope was the Antichrist. In later years he realized that the stain perdured long after he had changed his judgment on the point. Still, the *Apologia's* account of his long journey reads more like a legal brief than like a spiritual autobiography. Newman wrote it as a history of his *opinions*, and thus stressed reason more than imagination and feeling. Not only do imagination and feeling get short shrift, but the mention they do get is often negative in relation to reason. So, although Newman had expanded his understanding of reason beyond the narrow syllogistic model of rationalism, he still saw reason as over against imagination and feeling, which were not to be trusted. He wanted to follow reason.

In the *Apologia* Newman presented the nature of his conversion in a way that reflects his characterization of the Anglican view of "Truth" as "entirely objective and detached." There was, he writes, "a contrariety of claims between the Roman and Anglican religions [on the Faith and the Church], and the history of my conversion is simply the process of working it out to a solution."[72] Although he had had some latent notion of unrest and a sense of being on a journey for a number of years (he mentions 1829 and 1833), intellectually the conversion process began, Newman tells us, in the summer of 1839 when he saw himself reflected as Monophysite and later repeatedly heard the ringing of Augustine's "Securus judicat orbis terrarum." But, despite his misgivings about the Anglican Church's status, he still had serious problems with the Roman Church, so he carried on, and even published *Tract 90* asserting the validity of a Catholic interpretation of the Thirty-nine Articles.

When recounting the experiences of 1839 in the *Apologia*, Newman portrays the Monophysite episode as a "doubt" about "the tenableness of Anglicanism." He characterizes the Augustinian quotation as a powerfully vivid "impression" on his imagination, comparing it with Augustine's own "Tolle, lege,--Tolle, lege." He had to reflect on it, he writes, "to determine its logical value, and its bearing upon [his] duty."

But his immediate reaction to the "dreadful misgiving" arising from these experiences was a feeling of "dismay and disgust." As we have noted, however, Newman was "determined to be guided, not by [his] imagination, but by [his] reason." As a result, by the time he wrote his *Apologia* he claimed: "Had it not been for this severe resolve, I should have been a Catholic sooner than I was." This is the point in the *Apologia*, as we have seen, at which Newman relates his realization of the big question, "What was I to do?" Then he writes: "I had to make up my mind for myself, and others could not help me." The phrase "make up my mind" conveys Newman's intended stress on reason. The words "for myself" suggest an independence of mind, one of the structural characteristics of cognitive conversion. And the concluding "others could not help me" emphasizes this independence. We must wonder, whether, twenty-five years after the fact, Newman overemphasizes his independence as well as the role reason would eventually play in his conversion, and whether, perhaps, he underestimates the role "others" would play. In any case, his words present the issue as a theological dilemma which called for an intellectual solution.[73]

One instance of Newman's determination to think for himself relates to his recognition that he had uncritically accepted views from the great Anglican Divines on the Roman Church, that he had taken their statements "for granted without weighing them for [himself]." In connection with his views on the Roman Church we also have the reason/imagination conflict about the Antichrist mentioned above. In the *Apologia* Newman tells us that, just before his Monophysite experience in 1839, he "underwent a great change of opinion" about the Vicar of Christ's stigmatization as the Antichrist, coming to believe that "such a calumny was almost one of the notes of the Church." But, he explains, "we cannot unmake ourselves or change our habits in a moment. Though my reason was convinced," he continues, "I did not throw off, for sometime after,—I could not have thrown off,—the unreasoning prejudices and suspicion, which I cherished about her at least by fits and starts, in spite of this conviction of my reason." Despite the meddling of "charitable Catholics," he was "'determined upon taking [his] time.'"[74] Newman's understanding of the reason/imagination relationship in this instance, where his reason preceded imagination, may offer a useful model for our later consideration of his long and difficult struggle of conversion to Rome. The major decision at the heart of such a conversion involves the whole person, of affective

imagination as well as reason, not just reason alone. Newman's resolve
to be guided by reason certainly prolonged his journey, as he claims.
However, later in this chapter I will argue that for at least the last
two years of his journey he had all the reasons he needed in place but
lacked the sufficient support of his affective imagination as well as the
pressure of external events necessary to motivate his difficult decision.

NEWMAN'S ANGLICAN DEATHBED

At the beginning of the *Apologia's* penultimate chapter, Newman famously writes: "From the end of 1841, I was on my death-bed, as regards my membership with the Anglican Church, though at the time
I became aware of it only by degrees." At a deathbed, he says, "the end
is foreseen"; it is only "a matter of time." But for the next two years, till
his 1843 resignation of St. Mary's, he tells us, he "never contemplated
leaving the Church of England (though he "expected or intended gradually to fall back into Lay Communion") because he "could not go to
Rome, while she suffered [inappropriate] honours to be paid to the
Blessed Virgin and the Saints."[75]

Though the end may be foreseen, the passage of time to it can be
excruciating. Not all of Newman's younger allies in this phase of the
Movement appreciated that "Great acts take time," as he puts in the
Apologia. Many urged him on with strong logical arguments. But
Newman was not impressed by "paper logic," because "there is a great
difference between a conclusion in the abstract and a conclusion in the
concrete." He quotes St. Ambrose's maxim, "Non in dialecticâ com-
placuit Deo salvum facere populum suum" ("Not by logic was God
pleased to save his people.") Newman was not "carried" on by logic, he
says, anymore than the weather is changed by "the quicksilver in the
barometer." Change is complex. "Pass a number of years," he says, "and
I find my mind in a new place; how?" Clearly, for Newman, it is not by
abstract logic. "It is the concrete being that reasons; ... the whole man
moves; paper logic is but the record of it." Thinking back to the Oriel
common room, he says, "One is not at all pleased when poetry, or elo-
quence, or devotion, is considered as if chiefly intended to feed syllo-
gisms." He sums up his view of logic and his circumstances in one classic sentence with a characteristic analogy. First he makes his point: "All
the logic in the world would not have made me move faster towards
Rome than I did"; then the image: "as well might you say that I have
arrived at the end of my journey, because I see the village church before

me, as venture to assert that the miles, over which my soul had to pass before it got to Rome, could be annihilated, even though I had been in possession of some far clearer view than I then had, that Rome was my ultimate destination."[76] So, one thing at least seems clear: though Newman wished to go by reason, it was not the shallow reason of abstract logic, but the deep reason of the full, concrete person. Just how this deep reason is related to affective imagination remains to be seen.

In a "state of serious doubt" about the Anglican Church, Newman resigned his St. Mary's living in September 1843, retiring into lay communion at Littlemore as an Anglican. Although he had a "probable prospect" of turning to Rome some day, he could not do it while he thought what he did of "the devotions she sanctioned to the Blessed Virgin and the Saints." Because he could not know what would come of his doubt, he did not give up his Oriel fellowship at that point.[77]

CERTITUDE AND PROBABILITY

Over against his doubt, Newman sought certitude, which he understood "as the consequence ... of the accumulative force of certain given reasons which, taken one by one, were only probabilities." In the *Apologia*, speaking about himself in 1843-1844, Newman asserts: "that I believed in a God on a ground of probability, that I believed in Christianity on a probability, and that I believed in Catholicism on a probability," and, he continues, "that these three grounds of probability, distinct from each other of course in subject matter, were still all of them one and the same in nature of proof, as being probabilities— probabilities of a special kind, a cumulative, a transcendent probability but still probability ... ." Unlike the "rigid demonstration" of mathematical certitude, in religious inquiry we "arrive at certitude by accumulated probabilities," a certitude which, with God's help, "rises higher than the logical force of our conclusions."[78]

At this point in the *Apologia*, Newman distinguishes between opinion and conviction. By 1843, Newman states clearly, his religious opinions had changed: "On the one hand I came gradually to see that the Anglican Church was formally in the wrong, on the other that the Church of Rome was formally in the right"; furthermore, he continues, "that no valid reasons could be assigned for continuing in the Anglican, and again that no valid objections could be taken to joining the Roman." Given that, he adds: "I had nothing more to learn; what still remained for my conversion, was, not further change of opinion, but to change opinion itself into the clearness and firmness of intellectual conviction."[79]

By "intellectual conviction" here Newman clearly means certitude. For, after going on to explain the two practical steps he took in 1843—the Retraction of his hard statements against the Roman Church and the resignation of his St. Mary's living, he immediately says in the *Apologia*: "I had one final advance of mind to accomplish, and one final step to take." And he explains this quite explicitly: "That further advance of mind was to be able honestly to say that I was *certain* of the conclusions at which I had already arrived." And, finally, based on this, "That further step, imperative when such certitude was attained, was my *submission* to the Catholic Church." But at this point in the *Apologia* Newman defines certitude not as "accumulated probabilities," but as a "reflex action; it is to know that one knows." In 1843 he was not near certitude, and did not reach it, he claims, "till close upon" his reception into the Catholic Church. He was in a state of painful doubt, in which he felt he could not continue. In the *Apologia* he describes his difficulty plainly. "I had been deceived greatly once; how could I be sure that I was not deceived a second time?" Again: "I thought myself right then; how was I to be certain that I was right now?" And again, with even greater intensity: "How many years had I thought myself sure of what I now rejected? how could I ever again have confidence in myself?" He repeats his understanding of certitude: "To be certain is to know that one knows"; and then poses the pointed question: "what inward test had I, that I should not change again, after that I had become a Catholic?" He realized that his misgivings needed a limit: "I must do my best and then leave it to a higher Power to prosper it." So, in late 1844 he resolved to write an essay on doctrinal development: and "if, at the end of it, my convictions in favour of the Roman Church were not weaker, of taking the necessary steps for admission into her fold." He would resolve what he regarded as an intellectual problem by turning to an intellectual means, by writing an essay. And his "test" would not be that his convictions become stronger, simply "not weaker."[80]

Newman was searching for certitude in a terribly troubled state. In a November letter to Manning he states his "paramount reason for contemplating a change": "my deep, unvarying conviction that our Church is in schism, and that my salvation depends on my joining the Church of Rome." And this "conviction remains firm under all circumstances, in all frames of mind." Added to this conviction is the growing "most serious feeling" that the reasons for his Anglo-Catholic belief "*must* lead [him] to believe more—and not to believe more is to fall back into scepticism." But this firm, deep, unvarying conviction is not enough. He is held back by a fear that he is "under a delusion." And his state of mind is all the more troubled when he thinks of how much he would be giving up in such a change, of "sacrifices irreparable, not only from [his] age, when people hate changing, but from [his] especial love of old associations and the pleasures of memory." And on the other side he had nothing in human terms to attract him: "no visions whatever of hope, no schemes of action," and, perhaps most importantly, "no existing sympathies with Roman Catholics"; he knew no Roman Catholics, he writes, and did not like what he heard of them. Humanly speaking, he was losing everything dear to him, and gaining nothing. And he was not "conscious of any feeling, enthusiastic or heroic, of pleasure in the sacrifice"; he had no affective support for the decision that confronted him.[81]

CONSCIENCE AND DUTY

At this point in the *Apologia* Newman also quotes from a series of letters he wrote to Maria Giberne at the end of 1844 and during the first half of 1845. In the first of these letters, in November, Newman seems ambivalent. He begins: "I am still where I was—I am not moving." Unlike many others, he says, he does not think a move is "either suitable or likely." But then, in the very next sentence, he says, "I have very little reason to doubt about the issue of things. But the when and how are known" only to Him. Here, again, he stresses that he has "a great dread of going merely by [his] own feelings, lest they should mislead [him]." He notes the great force of the opinions and feelings about him that exist "on every side and among all parties." Still, "By one's sense of duty one must go, but external facts support one in doing so." Two months later, in January, after noting the unsatisfactory state of the Roman Catholics, Newman makes a clear assertion: "This I am sure of, that nothing but a simple, direct call of duty is a warrant for anyone leaving our Church … ." No attraction to the Roman Church, no repulsion for the Anglican counts. "The simple question is," he insists, "Can *I* (it is personal, not whether another, but can *I*) be saved in the English Church? am I in safety, were I to die to-night? is it a mortal sin in me, not joining another Communion?" Clearly, Newman is now in the radical realm of personal conscience. And less than three months later, at the end of March, he makes an explicit reference to conscience as he recasts his dilemma once more. "My own convictions are as strong as I suppose they can be," he says, "only it is so difficult to know whether it is a call of *reason* or of *conscience*. I cannot make out if I am impelled by what seems to me clear, or by a sense of *duty*." He stresses "how painful this doubt is," and how he is waiting, "hoping for light," though he realizes he has "no right to wait for ever for this." Surprisingly, perhaps, he adds that he "would attend to any new feelings" he might have as a result of the prayers of his friends. And then he refers to his move as practically a foregone conclusion, indicating that he probably will not last, as he had hoped, until the summer of 1846, seven years from his first convictions, but intended to give up his Oriel fellowship in October and then publish an explanation of his move before Christmas. In fact, as we saw above, his "difficulties so cleared away" as he worked on his *Essay* that he "resolved to be received" before finishing it.[82]

Reflecting on his move to the Roman Catholic Church in his *Apologia*, Newman says that he had no "trouble about receiving those additional [Roman] articles," like Transubstantiation, as soon as he believed, upon his conversion, that "the Roman Catholic Church was the oracle of God ... ." He acknowledges "intellectual difficulties," but asserts, famously, that "Ten thousand difficulties do not make one doubt ... ." Those "additional articles" notwithstanding, Newman sums up the effect of his move to Rome in extremely low-key, minimal terms: "I was not conscious to myself, on my conversion, of any change, intellectual or moral, wrought in my mind." He continues: "I was not conscious of firmer faith in the fundamental truths of Revelation, or of more self-command; I had not more fervour; but it was like coming into port after a rough sea ... ."[83]

Newman had been on a "rough sea" from the summer of 1839 until October 9, 1845. During those six years he had moved from his first doubt about the "tenableness of Anglicanism" to his final decision to be received into the Roman Catholic Church. In his contemporaneous letters and in his retrospective *Apologia*, Newman explains those years of struggle as an intellectual process of striving for certitude. He knew the process would be lengthy, but he was determined to be guided by reason, not by affective imagination. He realized that he had to make up his own mind for himself, but he was also aware that others—especially his younger colleagues—had influence on him, and that whatever he finally did would influence many others.[84]

Conversion may be a rather private and compartmentalized event for some people, but not for Newman. However much he would have preferred privacy during this deeply personal process, he was, in fact, in a fishbowl, with what must have seemed like the whole world watching him, taking notes, and expressing opinions. In addition to that social pressure, Newman also realized that what he characterized as an intellectual process would not be isolated in its consequences. For him going over to Rome would not simply mean holding different religious opinions and attending a different church for Sunday services. It would mean that every aspect of his whole world would change: his Anglican career, colleagues, friends, even family relationships would be permanently lost. All this made for an incredibly complex and painful process, stretched out over years, and marked by confusion, ambivalence, and ambiguity. It is no wonder that contemporary commentators as well as later historians found much to criticize.

THREE MORE BLOWS, AND MONASTIC DESIRE

Among Newman's critics, Frank Turner is the most recent historian to challenge Newman's account of his conversion process. We have already seen Turner's claim that Newman's real target as a Tractarian had been Evangelicalism, not Liberalism. Turner sees Newman's conversion less as the positive culmination of an intellectual and spiritual development than as the negative result of Newman's failure to effect a Catholic transformation of the Anglican Church. He summarizes his view: "The entrance of Newman into the Roman Catholic Church itself was the collapse of a whole series of social and ecclesiastical relationships that had permitted him to remain in the English Church despite his sectarian tendencies." Indeed, he continues, "Newman delayed his decision to be received into the Roman Catholic Church for as long as possible, and in the end found that decision largely forced upon him ... ."[85]

Turner cites three external events of 1845 as a second set of sharp blows received by Newman, "even more crushing to his situation in the English Church than the autobiographically more famous ones of 1841." The first of these three blows, noted above, was the failed attempt by the College Heads, in February, to have *Tract 90* condemned by University Convocation along with W. G. Ward's *The Ideal of a*

Christian Church. Though Newman's friend R. W. Church, a proctor, vetoed the censure of *Tract 90*, the effort at condemnation was a clear sign to Newman that he was to be persecuted even in the passive existence of his Littlemore retreat. The second external blow came in June with the censure of Frederick Oakeley by the ecclesiastical Court of Arches. Oakeley, one of the newer, stronger Tractarians, who had stood with Ward, had then gone on to publicly claim the right to hold Roman doctrine while subscribing to the Thirty-nine Articles. Oakeley's position was more radical than Newman's, but its repudiation could be understood to extend to Newman's more moderate position and the principles of *Tract 90.* In Turner's view, after the Oakeley decision the position that Newman and his followers "hoped to realize over time had become legally, if not necessarily theologically, untenable." Finally, in late September, there occurred a third event which Turner thinks *may* have been another blow to Newman: the death of the bishop of Bath and Wells, with the prospect of Oxford's Bishop Bagot being transferred to Bath and Wells to succeed him. Though this transfer was not publicly announced until October 16th, Turner considers it likely that it could have been known in Oxford early enough to have influenced Newman's decision "to enter the Roman Church when he did." Turner's point is that as bishop of Oxford Bagot had been somewhat protective of the Tractarians, and that Newman was well aware that, in contrast, any new bishop Peel might appoint to Oxford would be less than favorable to the Tractarians. Maybe this prospect, according to Turner, was the sign to Newman that it was time to go while the going was, though never good, at least better than it was likely to soon become.[86]

Beyond these three specific external events, however, there lies, in Turner's interpretation of Newman's conversion, one major reality: Newman's fundamental desire to live in a monastic community of celibate men, of devoted followers. In this account, Newman's move to Rome was finally precipitated by the conversions to Roman Catholicism of several of his younger Littlemore colleagues. Newman's desire to maintain his monastic community was so strong that he followed his younger colleagues in order to continue monastic life with them in the Roman Catholic Church.[87] By going over to Rome despite everything Newman did to keep them in the Anglican Church, Newman's younger followers turned the tables in their relationship to him, and in the end the leader became the follower. Whatever validity this interpretation of Newman's motivation may have, it does highlight how significant communities of unmarried men had been in his adult life—from the single tutors and students at Oriel to the celibate Tractarian colleagues at monastic Littlemore. As important as family, friends, and colleagues were to Newman, monastic celibacy—first Anglican, then Roman—was his priority, and finally Newman left the married Keble and Pusey and followed the celibate Dalgairns and others to Rome.

TRUTH IN AMBIGUITY

My purpose here is not to present Newman's conversion in terms of black or white interpretations. My aim is a balanced interpretation, acknowledging the interpersonal, social, and political context, while also recognizing the profoundly intellectual and spiritual reality of Newman's conversion. Truth here, as in most complex human realities, lies in ambiguity. My point is that we can understand the many years of misery and confusion Newman suffered before his conversion only if we appreciate the *fully* personal reality of his struggle. Though intellectual and spiritual, the struggle was anything but abstract and rarified. It was deeply embedded in the affective and imaginative dimensions of a very complicated individual, and it was carried out in a highly complex social and political world. With that proviso stated, we can now turn again to consider the course that, in retrospect, the author of the *Apologia* and we know ended in Rome, but that to the Tractarian Newman must have seemed for its greater part less like a journey—even an extremely arduous journey—to a known destination along a clearly marked road with the aid of a map and compass, and more like the stumbling steps of a lost person's unaided groping through a thick forest on a dark night. By the 1840s Newman was lost in confusion; he knew what he wanted, but he did not trust himself to go for it; he knew he had been wrong before.

We have seen Newman's version of his half dozen years before the conversion to Rome—through his contemporaneous letters as well as his retrospective *Apologia*. It is essentially the story of an intellectual search for certitude about the true church. If he began negatively with doubts about the Anglican Church, before too long—determined to go by reason and not by affective imagination—he came positively to the opinion that the true church was in Rome. He held this opinion for much of this pre-conversion period. But it was only an opinion.

He needed to turn this opinion into a clear and firm intellectual conviction. He had been greatly deceived before when he thought he was right. How could he be certain he was right now? What inward test could assure that he would not change again? He needed certitude. He needed, as he put it, to know that he knew. Finally, his test took a negative form: he would work his way intellectually through the issue of doctrinal development, and if at the end of that task his favorable opinion of the Roman Church was not weaker, he would take the necessary steps to conversion. He portrays the entire ordeal as an intellectual process, a process guided by reason, seeking not just opinion but certitude.[88]

THREE KEY PHASES

It may be that Newman understood himself as only seeking evidence to transform a merely hypothetical opinion into a definite judgment. But much of his language about certitude and degrees of conviction, as well as about affective imagination and conscience, suggests that his story needs some further analysis. I will proceed in this analysis of Newman's last six years as an Anglican by delineating three two-year phases, each culminating in a significant internal and external event: 1) by late 1841, after enduring the "three blows," he had affirmed his 1839 discovery that the *Via Media* was an "impossible idea" and had made plans to set up a community at Littlemore; 2) by late 1843 he had made a judgment of conscience that the Roman Catholic Communion is the Church of the Apostles and had resigned his St. Mary's living; and 3) by late 1845 he had decided to act in accord with his judgment of conscience, and had given up his Oriel fellowship and made, as he put it, his submission to the Roman Catholic Church. In summary: following upon his Monophysite discovery in 1839, Newman made 1) a *theoretical judgment* of truth (1841), then 2) a *practical judgment of conscience* about that theoretical judgment's personal rightness for himself (1843), and finally 3) a *decision* to act on that judgment of conscience (1845). Although Newman's conversion is usually identified narrowly with his 1845 decision, here I will interpret it more broadly as spanning some six years, 1839-1845, highlighted by key moments, and culminating in the decision of October 1845. We must now examine each phase of this lengthy conversion more closely.

Reflection and Judgment. First, there was the initial discovery, leading to doubt. In the *Apologia* Newman begins his conversion narrative with a simple, direct sentence: "The Long Vacation of 1839 began early." But the events of the next six years triggered during that Long Vacation would be anything but simple and direct. In the course of his study of the Monophysites that summer, Newman for the first time experienced a doubt about "the tenableness of Anglicanism." On top of that doubt, almost immediately came Augustine's "Securus judicat orbis terrarum." With that combination, "the theory of the *Via Media* was absolutely pulverized." But, as powerful as the summer's experiences had been, the thought that "The Church of Rome will be found right after all" soon vanished, and Newman's "old convictions remained as before." Or so it seemed; in fact, the doubt had been planted; Anglicanism would never again be the same for Newman. As we have seen, Newman mentions in the *Apologia* that for years he had had a latent notion that he was on a journey, that his "mind had not found its ultimate rest." He cites the 1833 Mediterranean trip, and even an 1829 experience of being "led on by God's hand blindly, not knowing whither He is taking me." But in those years he had not distrusted his own convictions; now in 1839 he did. What was he to do? He realized he had to make up his mind for himself; and he was determined to go by reason, not imagination. He knew it would take time; meanwhile it would be business as usual, or so he hoped. But, as we have seen, however the externals may have appeared, business was anything but usual in Newman's mind, as, in deep intellectual transition, he became "very nearly a pure Protestant," with no theology beyond his three propositions of 1833 (dogma, the sacramental system, and anti-Romanism).[89]

Publicly, Newman carried on the battle. *Tract 90* was published in February 1841, at which point he writes in the *Apologia*: "I was indeed in prudence taking steps towards eventually withdrawing from St. Mary's, and I was not confident about my permanent adhesion to the Anglican creed; but I was in no actual perplexity or trouble of mind." In the following months there was "immense commotion," but *Tract 90* was not condemned, and Newman thought he had weathered the storm. Then, in the summer, began the "three blows" of 1841. First it was the Monophysite ghost returning in the guise of Arians, and Newman's realization that the truth lay not in the *Via Media* but in Rome. Then the bishops began their attack on *Tract 90*. Finally, there was the Jerusalem Bishopric affair, which "finally shattered" Newman's faith in the Anglican Church. In Newman's retrospect, this was the "beginning of the end"; it put him on his Anglican deathbed.[90]

A month after his conversion to Rome, Newman wrote to a critic about his allegiance to the basic Anglican principles of Antiquity and Apostolical Succession, specifying three phases. "From the time I began to suspect their unsoundness," he wrote, "I ceased to put them forward." Later, "When I was fairly sure of their unsoundness, I gave up my Living." Finally, "When I was fully confident that the Church of Rome was the only true Church, I joined her."[91] Again, Newman is portraying his journey in purely intellectual terms, but his specification of phases is suggestive for our analysis.

By the end of 1841, when he fell on his Anglican deathbed, Newman had completed the first of these three phases. He had moved from his initial 1839 suspicion to a theological judgment: the truth was in Rome, not in the *Via Media*. The *Via Media* had "disappeared for ever," and a new, more subjective theory had taken its place: "the promised inward Presence of Christ with us in the Sacraments … ." This intellectual move, drawn out over two full years, had not been easy. Theoretical judgments, even those seeming to involve little or no self-reference, can be difficult and protracted.[92]

The process of reflective understanding preceding scientific judgment has recently been nicely characterized by the University of Toronto neurologist and geneticist Peter St. George-Hyslop: "We are aware of little bits of data as they come out that say, 'Yes, it's real,' but not very strongly, so what you get is not really a eureka moment but something that is incremental. It starts out," he says, "as 'Uh-huh, but it's probably a fluke,' to 'Maybe it's not a fluke,' to 'This could be real, let me see what I can do to make it go away,' to 'Well, it seems pretty robust, but there are still problems,' to 'We've taken this as far as we can and we concede that there are many things to be done on this story, but before we do too much more it needs to be put in the hands of some other people, with totally different data sets and totally different ways of analyzing things, and see if they get the same results.'"[93] If we transpose that process from a team of scientists quietly working together in a laboratory to a single theologian pondering a question of intense self-interest, and working increasingly alone but under sharp public scrutiny, with no one else to hand off to, we may perhaps begin to appreciate what Newman was facing during these two difficult years as he struggled toward judgment. And that was only the beginning.

If a pure, abstract intellectual judgment had been all he needed, Newman could have converted to Rome at the end of 1841. But, as we shall now see, much more was required. He had to move, in his words, from a "conclusion in the abstract" to a "conclusion in the concrete."[94]

Discernment and Judgment of Conscience. Having reached a theological judgment about the inadequacy of the basic Anglican principles and about the truth of Rome by the end of this first phase of relatively objective reflection, Newman entered what turned out to be a second two-year phase (1842-1843) of intense personal *discernment*: given his theological judgment that the Roman Church, not the Anglican, was the true church, what did that judgment mean for *him*, what should *he do* about it? This second phase moved the process from the more objective to the more subjective: now Newman was seeking not just the truth about the church, but the truth for him; he was struggling not just for a judgment of reason, but for a judgment of *conscience*. Conscience is the *self* struggling to discern what to do in a particular situation of moral value.[95] Judgments of conscience are thus first-person practical judgments aimed at action, and they carry a built-in moral demand: *this* is what *I must do* on pain of violating my very *self*. Judgments of conscience are therefore simultaneously both existential and practical; they involve the acting self as well as the world acted upon. Such judgments of conscience are acts of a "concrete being," as Newman would say, of a "whole man." Newman's theological judgment of reason against the Anglican principles and for the truth of Rome constituted a cognitive conversion of content. But because it was only an abstract, intellectual judgment without a personal, practical *terminus ad quem*, it left him hanging existentially in transitional perplexity and confusion, not knowing what to *do*. Now he needed to move to a judgment of conscience in order to establish a concrete personal objective, to set up the possibility of a positive, decisive *act*.

In this second phase, as we noted earlier, Newman moved into the Littlemore community with younger members of the Movement, engaged in correspondence with Roman Catholic Charles Russell, retracted his anti-Roman statements, and published his *University Sermons*, including his final St. Mary's sermon on doctrinal development, preached in February 1843. As one agonizing month followed another in 1843, finally he personally and existentially reached the explicit and positive judgment that the Church of Rome was the Church of the Apostles, the Catholic Church, and that the Anglican Church, because it was not in communion with Rome, was not part of the Catholic Church.[96] Finally, after months and months of personal discernment, the Catholic-minded Newman acknowledged that the Roman Church was the only and necessary alternative to the Anglican Church he now perceived as theologically bankrupt. Despite Rome's many problems, he now saw himself with the "extreme party." Whether he fully realized it at that point or not, this judgment was a judgment of conscience that required him to join the Roman Catholic Church. But that judgment requiring a move to Rome would have to be executed by a *decision*. And that decision, involving every dimension of Newman's being and every aspect of his situation, was so excruciatingly difficult that it would require another two years, two years of agonizing *deliberation*. All he could bring himself to in 1843 was the resignation from his St. Mary's living, which he did on September 7ᵗʰ, after one of the Littlemore community, William Lockhart, went over to Rome.

Deliberation and Decision. Regarding the third two-year phase of his ecclesial conversion's six painful years, Newman writes in the *Apologia* that what he needed was greater intellectual conviction, in a word, certitude. This view fits well with Newman's intellectual portrayal of his conversion as a search for a solution to a controversy. In this perspective, he had found the solution by the autumn of 1843; now he must become certain of it. But if certitude is, as Newman puts it, knowing that one knows, he would be facing an impossible quest. If certitude is, on his account of it, a second judgment that a first judgment is correct, he would be involved in an endless series of judgments. I am suggesting a different portrayal of this phase of his conversion. On my account of it, by the autumn of 1843 Newman had reached as much certitude as there was to be reached: he knew what he must do. The cognitional basis of this account is that certitude is not a second judgment, but a quality of a first judgment. In Newman's language, it is a satisfactorily high degree of probability, a probability intrinsic to the first judgment itself. Seeking certitude in a separate judgment is not only fruitless but encourages indecision and even, in the extreme, debilitating scrupulosity. But, if Newman knew what he had to do, he also knew how difficult what he must do would be, and that was the rub. He was right in thinking that "Great acts take time." The further time he needed, however, was not for greater certitude, but for sufficient motivation. He needed time to convince himself to decide to do what he knew had to be done. And because the obstacles he had to overcome in this course of *deliberation* were great, it is not difficult to understand that it took him the best part of two years to reach a decision. Even a clear, strong judgment of conscience that a change is right and necessary must overcome the existential drag of inertia working against deconversion. Deconversion is often extremely difficult. Even when one's present world is seriously problematic, it is still familiar and, in many ways, even easy, comfortable. Leaving it for a new, unknown, strange world can be enormously challenging.

Because Newman was by nature an intellectual, focused in the *Apologia* on his "religious opinions," it is understandable that he paid little attention to non-cognitive, existential obstacles in recounting his conversion. For the same reason it is not surprising that he chose to bring things to a head by writing his *Essay* on development, rehearsing once again a position he had been establishing for several years. He would resolve what he regarded as an intellectual problem with an intellectual argument. But the existential obstacles are exactly what must be understood if we are to appreciate the extremely difficult course of his conversion to the Roman Church, especially its last two-year phase of deliberation. We have seen that Newman was all too painfully aware of the losses a move to Rome would entail.

First, there was Newman's family. Having already lost his beloved youngest sister Mary and his parents to death, as well as his brothers to intolerance, the prospect of now losing Harriett and Jemima was overwhelming. Harriett was already alienated by his religious views, and Jemima upset by his resignation from St. Mary's. They could not be expected to understand a move to Rome; he could lose both for good.

Second, there were Newman's friends, who were especially important to him. He had already lost Froude, and recently Bowden, to death. He knew a move to Rome would cut him off from Keble and Pusey and his other Anglican friends and Tractarian colleagues, excepting only those who were going over themselves. Such a loss would be devastating. And with his friends and colleagues, he would also be losing Oxford. He was quintessentially an Oxford man, and now that identity would be gone forever. At every crucial point in his adult life, as we have seen, Newman had been influenced by one group or another of his Oxford friends. To a significant degree the very meaning of his self was rooted in his friendships, his independent stances not withstanding. Could he bear their loss?

This brings us, third, to the Anglican Church itself, *the* Church of England, the church Newman was born into and had grown up in. From boyhood, he had known no other. He loved the Anglican Church, and had devoted his life to it. It may be impossible for anyone else to appreciate how much it meant to him. For all his adult years, the Anglican Church had been his whole life. Everything he wrote, everything he did, was for the Anglican Church. Despite all the difficulty and grief he had experienced in it, it was his church. To leave it was almost unthinkable, but that was what he was now faced with, that was what he now knew he had to do.

Humanly speaking, the prospect of these losses of family, friends, and church was intolerable for Newman. And, again humanly speaking, there was nothing to attract him to the Roman Church. He knew little of it, and what he did know was anything but attractive. Newman was an Anglican, an Englishman through and through, and to him everything about the Roman Catholic Church was "foreign," one of a nineteenth-century Englishman's strongest epithets. Indeed, this was a church despised by Englishmen, a church whose pope Newman himself had thought was the Antichrist. And the Roman Church itself was not enjoying worldly power and glory at this point. Only faith could bring Newman to the point of seriously considering this church, but not even faith could erase the painful losses joining it would inflict on him. Because the true church meant salvation to him, such a dreadful decision was rending his self, his very being, and for a while left him immobile. It would probably have given Newman little consolation had he known that his fellow Englishman Charles Darwin was already well into a painful two-*decade* process of deliberation about publishing his own very different but not unrelated ideas on development. Anticipating great controversy and division, Darwin was finally able to end his own deliberation only with the help of an external event, the threat of a competitor's imminent publication.

Like Darwin or anyone else in such an unbearable situation, Newman needed a push, or, as he might say, an external sign. As we have seen, this push, in Turner's view, came in the form of a second set of three external blows in 1845 and, most importantly, in Newman's fundamental desire for monastic life. The three blows—the College Heads' attempt in February to have *Tract 90* condemned by Convocation, the censure of Oakeley by the Court of Arches in June, and likely the prospect in September of a new, less supportive bishop in Oxford—functioned principally as clear signs to Newman that he had finally lost the political battle for a Catholic form of Christianity within the Anglican Church. The twelve-year Tractarian campaign for Catholic faith in the Church of England was over, dead. If Newman did not know that before, he knew it now. His Anglican Church would not join Rome, and it would not sanction Catholic life within its walls. Newman did not want to leave his beloved church, but in 1845 it became all too evident that his church had no room for him. Deconversion was becoming an increasingly realistic possibility.

Finally, there was Newman's desire for monastic life—really as much a pull as a push. For a few years now he had had Littlemore, a community of young celibate men of strong Catholic leaning living on a monastic model. But now that community was breaking up, with members following Lockhart to the Roman Catholic Church. Littlemore had been Newman's last best hope for Catholic life within the Anglican Church. Now even that hope was disappearing. Although a move to Rome by Newman would entail severe losses, including his great friends from the early years of the Tractarian Movement, not moving would mean the loss of these younger members of his monastic community, of the community itself. Thus, the very departure of these converts worked to pull Newman toward Rome. Though impetuous to his cautious eye, these younger men would in fact provide him a known, welcoming social place in an otherwise mostly unknown and perhaps not so friendly Roman Church. In these converts he could anticipate in the Roman Church a continuation of his monastic community, a community not only of celibate men, but of young men devoted to him. In these converting companions Newman could *imagine* a place for himself in the Roman Catholic Church; he could *feel* personal support for a final step into the unknown. He now had the affective-imaginative strength to follow through and act on his judgment of conscience. One can only guess—we cannot know—what Newman would have done absent the push of the 1845 blows or the pull of his younger converting colleagues. But, in human terms, without these influences it is difficult to imagine him doing what he did—going over to Rome. As he would put it, external facts were supporting his sense of duty.[97] To be clear on this basic point: although Turner sees the three blows of 1845 and the desire for monastic life as motivating Newman's conversion to the Roman Church, I am interpreting them rather as pushing Newman's deconversion *from* the Anglican Church. Newman clearly had other positive intellectual and spiritual reasons motivating his conversion *to* Rome.

CONCLUSION

So, while Newman was writing his intellectual justification of his ecclesial conversion through the months of 1845, various existential factors jointly came to a head, giving him the impetus he needed to bring his deliberation process to a decision. For Newman conversion to the Roman Catholic Church was fundamentally a matter of personal salvation. But Newman, like the rest of humankind, had mixed motives. The ambiguity of his conversion raised many questions among his contemporary and later critics. Still, to acknowledge that his conversion, like all others, was embedded in a matrix of personal existential human factors does not diminish or in any way detract from its profound spiritual authenticity. In the midst of his long struggle to bring the Anglican Church to a recognition of its Catholic spirit, Newman by late 1841 had come to the clear acknowledgement, in an *abstract theological judgment*, that the true Catholic Church was the Roman, not the Anglican. By the end of 1843, after two years of personal discernment, he then broke through the murky confusion of his own situation and came to the existential realization, in a *concrete judgment of conscience*, that *he* must join the Roman Catholic Church, that his salvation depended on converting to it. As difficult as it had been to reach that judgment, he then had to bring himself to execute it. Finally, after two more years submerged in excruciating separation angst, he was able—with the various forms of push and pull we have noted—to overcome the painful obstacles of his personal situation and terminate his deliberation process in a definitive *decision* to leave the Anglican Church (deconversion) and to join the Roman Catholic Church (conversion), to seek, as he puts it, "admission into the One Fold of Christ."

Newman had been determined to be guided by reason, not by imagination. He thought he needed greater conviction, certitude. In fact, all along he had been guided by reason, and, at least by 1843, he had as much certitude as one can have in personal value judgments. He did not need, and could not have had, more certitude. What he needed, rather, was the strength of affective imagination to effect the decision his conscience was demanding. Rather than guard against imagination by reason, he needed to be moved by it. He needed to *feel* free to leave everything in his life connected with the Anglican Church, and to *imagine* his way forward into the unknown of the Roman Church. By October 1845 he felt he could imagine that way.

Thus the six-year course of Newman's ecclesial conversion, which began with a seed of doubt about "the tenableness of Anglicanism" (1839), and then took root in two complementary judgments on the truth of the Roman Church (1841), and his duty in conscience to join it (1843), ended in a decision (1845) whose process of deliberation reached far deeper into the strata of his self than suggested by his intellectual portrayal of "the history of [his] conversion [as] simply the process of working [the controversy about the true church] out to a solution." Intellectually Newman believed in change, as he affirmed in his *Essay* on development. At the same time, by temperament he was a cautious man; he had a lot to lose, and he knew he had been wrong before. These two factors combined to produce the major change of ecclesial conversion, but only after six painful years of reflection, discernment, and deliberation. Though rooted in an intellectual judgment, Newman's ecclesial conversion is best understood as a moral (religious) decision responding to a judgment of personal conscience. It is to Newman's own understanding of conscience that we turn in the next chapter, after a consideration of his life as a Roman Catholic.

4. THE ROMAN CATHOLIC NEWMAN AND CONSCIENCE

1. FROM LITTLEMORE TO BIRMINGHAM, AND BACK AND FORTH TO DUBLIN

LITTLEMORE, OSCOTT, AND ROME

Despite the enormous life change effected by Newman's October 1845 ecclesial conversion to the Roman Catholic Church, Littlemore continued to be his "port." He knew he could not remain there indefinitely, but Littlemore had been such a peaceful refuge during the recent stormy years that he found it difficult to leave. When you have turned away from everything in your life, as he had, where do you go? Newman's answer came when Nicholas Wiseman, the president of Oscott College near Birmingham, invited him and the other Oxford converts to stay at the Old Oscott. Newman finally brought himself to leave Littlemore late in February 1846, taking with him a conviction to be ordained a Roman Catholic priest. He did not find life particularly pleasant at Oscott, despite the consolation he took from the reservation of the Blessed Sacrament in the chapel. By September he and his colleague Ambrose St. John were off to Rome to prepare for ordination at the College of Propaganda, where they were received as something of celebrities. Before long they were even accorded a welcoming audience by Pope Pius IX himself. Newman was impressed by the austere life of the college's Jesuit faculty, if not by their theology (but on this latter point the feeling was mutual; and Newman had to devote considerable time to defending his ideas on development and the relationship between faith and reason). He considered the possibility of joining a religious order like the Dominicans or the Jesuits (earlier he had been very taken by Ignatius of Loyola's *Spiritual Exercises*), but rather quickly decided that they were not exactly what he had in mind for the next phase of his life.

THE ORATORIAN PRIEST

With the Oratory of St. Philip Neri—a *via media* between the dioc-
esan priesthood and the religious orders—Newman found the possibility of continuing the Littlemore community into his new Roman
Catholic life. There would be a rule, but no vows, and by a papal
Brief he would be the new English Oratory's superior. Newman was
ordained at the end of May 1847, and before long was off to Santa
Croce for a few months of prayer and domestic chores at the Roman
Oratory's novitiate, where he and Ambrose St. John were joined by
other Oxford converts. Surprisingly, his spiritual life was not thriv-
ing at this point. Perhaps it was exhaustion from the battering he had
taken during the Tractarian years, or a letdown after the difficult lead-
up to his ordination, but for whatever reason he lacked the enthusiasm
about the priesthood and Oratorian life one might expect. He was experiencing what can only be characterized as depression.[1] In any case,
by the end of 1847 he was back at Oscott (now re-named Maryvale)
as an Oratorian priest, and began the New Year and a new phase of his
life by saying Mass there for the first time on January 1, 1848.

Not many months passed before the anonymous appearance of
Newman's novel *Loss and Gain*, the quasi-autobiographical story of
his Anglican hero Charles Reding's conversion to the Roman Catholic
Church. Otherwise, most of Newman's time and energy went into
the establishment of the new Oratory—involving difficult community politics especially aggravated by convert F. W. Faber's joining the
Oratory along with members of his own community of St. Wilfrid's,
also near Birmingham. Within the first year of its existence, Newman's
Maryvale community moved to St. Wilfrid's, briefly, and then, in
January 1849, to the urban setting Newman had originally desired—
in a "gloomy gin distillery" on Alcester Street, Birmingham,[2] where
they stayed for three years before moving in early 1852 to a newly
constructed Oratory in Edgbaston outside the city. Faber's community
remained at St. Wilfrid's for a few months, before establishing its own
Oratory in London, which became increasingly independent (and
formally separated in October 1850) as it shared little of Newman's
interest in things intellectual or educational.[3]

In the spring of 1850 the London Oratory invited Newman to
give a series of lectures. The Privy Council conveniently provided a
topic for the lectures when, in the Gorham case, it ruled, in effect,

that baptismal regeneration was not an essential Anglican doctrine, thus driving a large number of converts on their way to Rome. Among them was Newman's friend Henry Edward Manning, the future Cardinal Archbishop of Westminster. From May to July Newman delivered his lectures on *Certain Difficulties Felt by Anglicans in Catholic Teaching*, a tough-minded critique of the Anglican Church addressed to Anglo-Catholics. Using imagination guided by reason, he argues by analogy that the Roman Catholic Church is the church of the Fathers, the real church, and that the national, liberal Anglican Church, an unreal fantasy, is no more than a dead Erastian branch. He loves his erstwhile Anglican brethren by calling a spade a spade. Anticipating his *Apologia*, he credits his life-long love of the early church Fathers for his conversion to Rome.[4]

If in *Difficulties* Newman went to the aid of Anglo-Catholics, the next year in his *Lectures on the Present Position of Catholics in England* he went after Protestant Anglicans for their bigotry against Catholics. Here he employs a rich assortment of imagery to demonstrate the poverty of the Protestant imagination. But in the course of this attack on Protestant prejudice Newman repeats serious accusations made by Wiseman against the Protestant convert Giacinto Achilli, a former Dominican priest condemned by the Roman Inquisition for sexual transgressions. In return Achilli, in the anti-Catholic climate of the day, had criminal charges brought against Newman for libel. The attempt to produce evidence on Newman's behalf was botched, and Newman found himself embroiled in court proceedings for more than a year. Finally, at the end of January 1853, with a possible prison sentence hanging in the balance through the many suspenseful months of legal maneuverings, the jury's verdict of June 1852 against Newman was upheld on appeal. That the sentence was a fine of merely £100 was a great relief for Newman and viewed as a moral victory.[5]

THE UNIVERSITY RECTOR IN DUBLIN, AND HIS IDEA

Beginning in April 1851, the possibility of a new Catholic University of Ireland entered Newman's life in the form of a letter from Archbishop Cullen of Armagh (of Dublin in 1852). The archbishop's initial request for advice and a "few lectures on education" led by the end of the year to Newman's appointment as rector-president of the proposed university.[6] (The university, encouraged by Rome, would be a Catholic alternative to the new Queen's University, in which Rome had forbidden

Catholic involvement.) Over the course of a month beginning on May 10, 1852 Newman delivered five lectures in Dublin, which later became the first, theological section of *The Idea of a University*. The lectures were well-attended and warmly received, though Newman had been anxious about not knowing his audience. This was the Ireland, to be sure, whose population had been reduced by a quarter through death and emigration since the Potato Famine first struck in 1845, the year of Newman's conversion to Rome.

Although heading up the university project would mean spending much time in Dublin away from his Oratorian community, Newman was initially very enthusiastic about his position, seeing it as something of a continuation in different circumstances of his years of struggle in Oxford.[7] He was warmly welcomed in Dublin, but his eagerness to get the project underway was not shared by the Irish bishops, who were not united in their support. The proposal of a Catholic university had come from Rome, but had found little enthusiasm among various clerical, social-economic, and political groups of Irish Catholics. And once Newman had been appointed rector, communication between him and Archbishop Cullen became very difficult. Indeed, Newman found himself in the middle of episcopal intrigue of a Roman kind unfamiliar to him. Newman was to be rector, but Cullen was to be in control. Among their many differences over administrative appointments, choice of site, selection of faculty, etc., perhaps Newman's desire to have lay control of university finances was the most important. Added to this was talk of the possibility that, to strengthen the rector's authority, Newman would be made a titular bishop. Wiseman had proposed the plan to the pope, along with the idea of a papal Brief formally establishing the university. But Cullen, though initially appearing to favor the elevation, quickly moved behind the scenes to scuttle it. He had sought Newman's name and expertise for the university, but Newman with episcopal authority was more than he was willing to deal with. So, without any mention of a bishopric, the papal brief Wiseman had requested was issued in March 1854, instructing the Irish bishops to establish the university, which they did in synod that May. Finally, then, three years after Cullen's first contact with him, Newman was formally installed as rector on June 4, 1854. The university began classes later that fall, with some twenty students and the expectation of more. Newman gave the inaugural lecture, "On the place held by the Faculty of Arts in the University Course," on November 9, 1854.

By June 1856, when Newman again met with the synod of Irish bishops, the university still had fewer than a hundred students. But the bishops approved Newman's plans for another three years. Newman was satisfied with the university's progress, but problems persisted—the clergy were less than enthusiastic, and the laity with money were less than supportive. He felt that the university needed new leadership to look toward the future, someone who would mix in society, dine out every night, and behave, as he put it in the language of Jane Austen, "condescendingly to others"—preferably a young Irish bishop.[8] In April 1857, fed up with the bishops' absolutism, he sent letters to Cullen and the other bishops announcing his resignation as of the next academic year. Cullen tried to persuade him to stay for three more years, but bargaining over the appointment of a vice-rector and other matters came to very little more than a short extension of his stay. So, on November 4, 1858, after giving three final lectures on consecutive days, Newman left Dublin for the last time. A week later he mailed his formal resignation, seven years after his first appointment.

Although the university was not a great success until later reconstituted as University College Dublin, Newman's involvement provided occasions for several lectures over the years which, as published, became one of the great and lasting contributions to Catholic education: *The Idea of a University*. The *Idea* is in two parts. The first part approximates the lectures Newman wrote in 1852, some for delivery in Dublin in response to Cullen's request, others for publication along with the Dublin lectures. In accord with Cullen's wishes, the lectures in this first part principally address the relationship between education and religion, or what Newman called "the great subject of the connection of religion with literature and science."[9] The second part consists of occasional lectures on particular related topics delivered at the university between 1854 and 1858.

Newman's plan for the new Dublin institution was a combination of the strengths of the English college tutorial system and the best of the European university professorial system.[10] Analogously, he would unite in one institution a focus on study of the classics with a context of universal knowledge provided by the many disciplines. Within the circle of disciplines theology would be first among equals. Still, Newman's educational key was the imperial intellect's philosophical view that would both order the relationship among the disciplines for the university and be the goal of a truly liberal education for the individual student. The liberally educated person would not know everything, but would know how everything fits together, would have a comprehensive view of all the disciplines. For Newman, now of the Roman persuasion, that philosophical view, of course, was Catholic Christian. An important example of the philosophical view at work is the way Newman distinguishes and relates religion and science as two separate worlds stemming from two different ways of knowing. Each is given its due, but neither is allowed to encroach on the other. At bottom, however, there is for Newman a unity of truth, and that unity is rooted in God.

The rectorship of the university had required Newman to spend much time in Dublin, away from his Birmingham Oratory, where all was not well. The departure of Faber's group to their own Oratory in London had merely relocated, not resolved, the tensions between the two groups, and between Newman and Faber.

FABER AND ORATORIAN POLITICS

A specific new problem, which Newman learned of in the fall of 1855, involved the London Oratory's application to Rome for some flexibility regarding the prohibition in the English Oratory's rule of providing spiritual direction for nuns. Newman, the author of the rule, was especially concerned. Any approval of change in the rule would affect not only London, but Birmingham as well. And the specific point at issue would change the character of the Oratory in the direction of London's interpretation of Oratory life, more pastoral and devotional, less cultural and intellectual. The autonomy and independence of individual Oratories were at stake. Most of all, though, Newman took London's unilateral move, made without consulting him as English founder, as a personal affront. Communications between the Oratories, the bishops, and Rome exacerbated rather than mollified the tensions. Newman felt at best isolated and ignored, at worst disrespected and attacked. "How odd it is," he thought, "all thro' life this is the sort of way I have been treated." A Roman rescript granting London's application had been issued in late 1855, but by the end of the year Rome assured Newman that its limited nature gave him no reason for concern. Still, Newman wanted greater clarity on the fundamental point of the autonomy of individual Oratories—that a Roman directive or rule interpretation for one Oratory would not affect another, at least not without full consultation. For this, a visit to Rome seemed necessary, and, losing no time, Newman arrived there in January 1856. After an audience with the pope and much consultation, in which Newman was advised that pressing his point would serve only to lessen his authority, including his power as *Deputato Apostolico* to establish new Oratories in England, he decided to withdraw his proposal, which, he learned, had led London to accuse him of an authoritarian move to establish himself as head of an Oratorian generalate in England. Despite the difficult complexities of the situation, he left Rome with a basic sense of contentment: "Every thing is turning out well—and I can never feel any thing but thankfulness and satisfaction that I have come here." Newman soon had doubts about the advice he had received, but the formalities of the Birmingham-London problem were officially settled later in the year by a final separation of the two Oratories and a foundation Brief from Rome for the London Oratory. The wounded feelings of the involved parties were not so easily or quickly healed.[11]

ECCLESIASTICAL POLITICS AND CONTROVERSIES

With the Achilli affair, the Irish university experience, and the London Oratory situation, the better part of the 1850s was for Newman a decade of anxiety and frustration. In the midst of all this, however, he managed to produce—in addition to *The Idea of a University*—lectures and essays on such topics as the history of the Turks, the Crimean War, and the history of universities. During the long vacation of 1855 he also completed *Callista*, a historical novel of conversion, first begun in 1848. More than an interesting story, *Callista* offers a comparison of the position of third-century Christians in the Roman Empire with nineteenth-century Catholics in England, an interpretation of conversion as developmental paralleling Newman's, and a view of conscience as transcendent, echoing the voice of the God of our deepest desire.[12]

Out from under the burden of the Irish university, and with the London Oratory controversy settled at least on paper, Newman looked forward to a year of peace and quiet in 1859. But that was not to be. Perhaps he was constitutionally unable to avoid difficulty and controversy.

The year had hardly begun when Newman found himself in the middle of a dispute between the bishops and the *Rambler*, the lay Catholic magazine. Döllinger and Acton, the two great liberal

Catholics of the time, had both written essays the bishops found objectionable—Döllinger linking Jansenism with Augustine, and Acton arguing for greater freedom of conscience. If the *Rambler* was to avoid condemnation, a new editor was needed, and Newman was the only person acceptable to both the bishops and the magazine people like Acton. Newman agreed to take the editorship, but before long he too became problematic, and his bishop encouraged him to resign, which he did, after only a few months in the position. His offence had been an editorial remark about the importance of the laity's opinion, and especially his use of the word "consult" in that context. So, as he was leaving the editorship, his parting shot was an essay titled "On Consulting the Faithful in Matters of Doctrine." In it, he not only explains his meaning of "consult" (inquiring about the fact of the laity's faith on some issue rather than asking for their judgment or opinion), but he also makes the case for such consultation: "because the body of the faithful is one of the witnesses to the fact of the tradition of revealed doctrine, and because their *consensus* through Christendom is the voice of the Infallible Church." Going on to claim that the laity were more reliable than the episcopacy during the Arian heresy won him no points with the bishops. Indeed, one of the bishops, Brown of Newport, sent a formal protest (delation) to Rome, complaining that Newman appeared to heretically contradict the doctrine of the church's infallibility. Fortunately for Newman, the issue was lost in the shuffle as the bishops and Rome consulted about it.[13]

As the 1860s began Newman found himself in the depths of depression. Not just recent events, but his entire time as a Catholic, indeed, his whole life seemed to be just one miserable string of failures, with few happy interruptions. Looking back over the decades, he dwelt on the worst experiences—his dismal performance on examinations at twenty, his loss of the Oriel tutorship at thirty, his Anglican ostracism over *Tract 90* at forty, his social disgrace over the Achilli judgment at fifty, and now his awkward place in the Catholic Church as he approached sixty. As for the future, he could only foresee a bleaker prospect as he anticipated the next decade. The great losses suffered at his conversion from Oxford to Rome had not been overcome, but only deepened, by his experiences as a Catholic, one disappointment after another, and suspicion rather than appreciation for his efforts. He battled with anger and despair, seeing himself as Sisyphus or Job.[14]

Newman did manage to resist public involvement when the issue of the pope's temporal power came to a head in 1861. And the next year he navigated the treacherous waters of intellectual freedom and authority in the church following upon Bishop Ullathorne's censure of the *Rambler* and its successor the *Home and Foreign Review*. But the censure made him wonder if he could ever write again without inciting great controversy. He was definitely feeling a tension between church authority and personal conscience.

Faber died in September 1863. Newman had visited him in London as he lay dying, asserting his love of Newman. The death ended an extremely difficult relationship, but not Oratorian troubles. For most of the past two years Newman had been trying to manage a crisis at the Oratory School, which had been established in Birmingham in 1859. A row had developed between Nicholas Darnell, the Oratorian Newman had appointed as headmaster, and Mrs. Wootten, the school's matron and a favorite of Newman's. Mrs. Wootten represented care for the boys' personal life that Newman wanted the school to emphasize. Darnell rejected Newman's attempt to effect a compromise with Mrs. Wootten, publicly resigned, and left the Oratory, taking some masters with him. Newman regarded any possible failure of the school as a disaster for the Oratory. He appointed Ambrose St. John as new headmaster and managed to put a staff together, but the burden was great, especially as it was added to the many daily Oratory responsibilities he had been forced to take on. He now had only six other members with him in the Birmingham Oratory. Given his low emotional state and the press of everyday duties, it is no wonder that he responded to rumors of his imminent return to the Anglican Church by admitting that his ordinary life as a Catholic was dreary, but no more dreary than his liturgical life as an Anglican had been. He would never leave the land of milk and honey of his Catholic faith to return to that religious desert.[15]

More often than not Newman felt useless: "So year goes on after year; and no one hires me."[16] He had to get up in the morning to attend to the endless mundane tasks; but there was nothing of importance for him. On at least one morning in 1863 he did not have the psychic energy to take his wake-up shower. Life was not good.

KINGSLEY AND THE *APOLOGIA*

Then, on the penultimate day of 1863, the mail arrived with a copy of the latest *Macmillan's Magazine*. Newman could not know how much his life was about to change. This anonymously forwarded issue contained a book review by a "C. K.," which included a totally gratuitous slam at Catholic priests and at Newman in particular: "Truth, for its own sake," the reviewer asserted, "had never been a virtue with the Roman clergy. Father Newman informs us," he continued, "that it need not, and on the whole ought not to be; that cunning is the weapon that Heaven has given to the saints," he snidely went on, "wherewith to withstand the brute male force of the wicked world which marries and is given in marriage. Whether his notion be doctrinely correct or not," he concluded, "it is at least historically so."[17]

Newman immediately protested to the publisher, and before long received a response from Charles Kingsley, the reviewer, defending his remarks. Views were exchanged, privately and publicly, but without the satisfaction Newman required. Finally, Newman decided that Kingsley, Anglican clergyman, novelist, and Regius Professor at Cambridge, was too important to let get away with this slander. After years of this kind of abuse from all directions, especially charges that he had been a secret papist during the years before his conversion, Newman was ready to use this opportunity to launch a major defense of his honesty and truthfulness. After collecting many of the letters he had written over the years, he summoned up a burst of energy and began to explain the development of his thinking from his boyhood to his conversion. In some two months of constant writing during the spring of 1864 he produced the eight parts of his *Apologia*, which first appeared as weekly pamphlets while he continued to write, then as a volume (then, again, after significant revision, in a second edition the next year).

After telling his story up to the 1845 conversion, Newman switched rhetorical gears, and, in what has ended up as the fifth and final chapter, turned to his thoughts as a Roman Catholic—from his conversion right up to the contentious issues of the day.

As to "fundamental truths of Revelation," Newman asserts that his conversion had brought about no change of mind. About particular peculiarly Roman Catholic doctrines, even difficult ones like Transubstantiation, which he had not previously held as an Anglican, he tells his readers that he had no difficulty in believing as soon as he "believed that the Roman Catholic Church was the oracle of God."[18] But how can one hold this belief; how can one affirm the church's infallibility? Here Newman counters belief in God with the evidence of a seemingly Godless human world. Something is fundamentally wrong in the world, and the distortion of reason away from religious truth is one of the principle effects of this radical human malady. Only an infallible church can resolve the conflict between errant reason and religious truth. And in this resolution reason is saved from its excesses, not destroyed, Newman argues, because reason and authority are not contradictory but mutually beneficial in their very conflict. (On the relationship of science and revelation, he demurs, as its history is short and its issues complex.) He quickly adds, of course, that, like reason, authority too can be abused. Likewise, in the area of religious truth, he is not excessively subtle in juxtaposing the contemporary Ultramontane view with the restraint the church had practiced over the centuries in the use of authority, allowing a creative and fruitful exercise of individual freedom. In his contemporary Catholic context, Newman positioned himself in the center, deliberately rejecting the extremes of Ultramontanism on the right and liberalism on the left. He was seeking some living space for his conscience in the church, an effort we will soon consider explicitly.

Finally, after defending Catholic clergy against the charge of mendacity, Newman concludes by dedicating his *Apologia* to the six remaining Birmingham Oratorians, Ambrose St. John in particular, who have been so faithful and sensitive to him over many years. They are the loyal ones who have sustained him through difficult times, the remnant of the community of celibate men, now not so young, he had always sought. In its effect, the *Apologia* did its job well, being met with much favor in many quarters, both Anglican and Roman, though, not surprisingly, failing to persuade Charles Kingsley.

OXFORD AND ROME REDUX

In the wake of the *Apologia's* popularity came the possibility of Newman returning to Oxford—the offer of a choice piece of property, and the suggestion from Bishop Ullathorne of establishing a mission church there. Newman had mixed feelings about returning to Oxford, but, with an eye to a future Oratory in Oxford, he decided to take up the bishop's suggestion. Ideas for a Catholic college or a residence for

Catholic students at the university soon complicated the picture, however, and by the end of 1864 the English bishops, spurred on by Rome and in particular by Manning, who did not want Newman's influence in Oxford, threw up a serious roadblock to Newman's return to Oxford by warning Catholics of the dangers of attending Protestant universities. Once again, Newman felt he had been done in by the hierarchy. Salt was rubbed into the wound when Newman soon found himself kneeling before Manning and kissing his hand at the latter's consecration as the new Archbishop of Westminster, only fourteen years after Manning's own conversion.

The Oxford plan was stalled, but not dead, at least in the mind of Bishop Ullathorne, who early in 1866 once again asked Newman to establish an Oxford mission church. By June the Birmingham Oratory agreed to take the mission on, but almost immediately complications arose again in Rome. Still, by the end of the year the bishop was able to tell Newman that Rome had given approval for an Oxford Oratory. What he did not tell Newman was that Rome was against having Newman in residence at Oxford, lest his presence encourage greater Catholic enrollment in the university. Unaware of this restriction, Newman engaged in preparations for the new Oratory until April 1867, when it was reported in the *Weekly Register* that the pope was against Newman going to Oxford, that only an Ultramontanist could be trusted with such a position. At that point Ullathorne finally told Newman about the secret Roman restriction on Newman of the previous year. The cat was now out of the hierarchical bag, and it was clear to Newman that he and his suspect views on points like the laity, hierarchical authority, and the pope's temporal power were the real obstacle to an Oratory in Oxford. And, if he was under an ecclesiastical cloud, he asked himself, could he really have any influence in Oxford anyway? And being the Ultramontanists' target, he knew there was reason to fear for the future of the Oratory School in Birmingham, and even of the Oratory itself. Before the end of the summer Newman gave Ullathorne his resignation from the Oxford project.

Despite his penchant for putting things in personal terms, Newman saw the attack on himself as having wider, more serious implications. If, he wrote to a supporter, "they are strong enough to put down me," for "not succumbing to the clique, no one else has a chance of not being put down, and a reign of terror has begun, a reign of denunciation, secret tribunals, and moral assassination"—"a formidable conspiracy

... against the theological liberty of Catholics," which he vowed to fight against.[19] The *Syllabus of Errors* had been promulgated at the end of 1864. In June 1867 the pope had announced his intention for a General Council; no one could say that papal infallibility would not be on its agenda.

During the past two decades the tables had completely turned on Newman. At his conversion in 1845 he had been the Anglicans' favorite whipping boy, and the darling of Roman Catholics. It was not long before his favored status in the Catholic Church began to gradually wither away over the years. In contrast, his 1864 *Apologia* in defense of his conversion had restored much of his good name among Anglicans, while adding to the growing suspicion of his views among his Catholic opponents, principally Archbishop Manning in England and the papal circle in Rome. The Oxford fiasco made those suspicions clear. Manning and Propaganda in Rome trusted Newman as little as he trusted them.

THE *GRAMMAR* AND INFALLIBILITY

During all the frustration of the Oxford business, Newman had taken a Swiss holiday in the summer of 1866. That vacation is notable for the intellectual breakthrough he made on a longstanding problem. As far back as his *Oxford University Sermons* he had been struggling with the relation of faith and reason, especially the issue of certitude. Finally, high in the Alps over Lake Geneva, he had a fundamental insight: "'You are wrong in beginning with certitude—certitude is only a kind of assent—you should begin with contrasting assent and inference.'"[20] That was the beginning of almost four years of intellectual labor that in 1870 finally resulted in his *Essay in Aid of a Grammar of Assent*. The complexity of the issue only partially explains the prolonged struggle, as Newman was not wanting for distractions during these years of work on the *Grammar*.

Late in 1867 Newman declined an invitation from the liberal French Bishop Félix Dupanloup to accompany him as his personal theologian to the upcoming council at the Vatican. But the council and its key issue of papal infallibility would not go away that easily.

Although Newman considered "the Pope's formal definitions of faith to be infallible,"[21] not as certain dogma, but as probable theological opinion, he was especially concerned about the negative effect all the talk about papal infallibility was having on converts and potential converts. Still, he again declined another invitation to attend the council, this one from the pope himself, through Bishop Ullathorne. Public activity, especially in Rome, just did not seem right for him; he preferred to work alone.

Newman thought there were more reasons against a formal definition than for one, but he was prepared to accept it as an article of faith if passed by the council. He viewed a definition as imprudent, not wrong. The church's judgment was the bottom line. His understanding of development was key. From the time of his conversion he had believed that "the present Roman Catholic Church is *the only Church* which is like, and it is very like, the primitive Church." Despite the fact that on an 1865 visit to John Keble's house he had not immediately recognized his old great friend after a twenty-year separation, Newman used an interesting analogy of personal recognition to make his point about the present Church of Rome: "It is almost like a photograph of the primitive Church; or at least it does not differ from the primitive Church near so much as the photograph of a man of 40 differs from his photograph when 20. *You know that it is the same man.*"[22]

Still, Newman recognized the great danger of papal infallibility being interpreted to extend beyond evolving the deposit of faith. But despite all his objections to the impending definition, his faith was with the church. And harkening back to the Augustinian theme of his conversion, he insisted particularly on the whole church's reception of papal and conciliar judgments—"securus judicat orbis terrarum."[23]

All his objections notwithstanding, Newman had decided against making any public statement. But he made his view clear in private letters. And in March 1870 a letter he had written to Bishop Ullathorne in Rome was publicly reported. In that letter, referring to the Ultramontanists, he had asked, in a string of rhetorical questions, "Why should an aggressive insolent faction be allowed to 'make the heart of the just mourn, whom the Lord hath not made sorrowful?'" If there had been any doubt about Newman's position the cat was now out of his own theological bag. After an immediate mistaken denial, Newman had to admit in a letter to the editor of the *Standard* that "aggressive insolent faction" was indeed his characterization of the Ultramontanists. And not entirely unhappy with the turn of events, he even used the occasion to furnish the editor with a copy of his letter to Ullathorne for publication.[24]

In July 1870 the Vatican Council proclaimed the definition of papal infallibility. Newman found its expression moderate enough, extending as it did only to faith and morals, and he had no trouble accepting it, though, as eighty bishops had left before the vote, there were questions about its validity. The Ultramontanists did not get the strong definition they had wanted, but Newman was particularly concerned about the precedent set by passing a dogma *"without definite and urgent cause"*: would this lead to an extension of the definition, encouraging popes to use their power without necessity? The Ultramontanists could be expected to continue their efforts to expand infallibility into such areas as science and politics. As Newman understood it, the pope's infallibility was the infallibility of the church, and no more. Infallibility was not a positive inspiration, but merely a negative gift protecting the pope from error. Given the definition of infallibility in July, Newman did not find the pope's surrender of Rome in September as entirely inappropriate. Perhaps it was too much for one man to be both infallible in things spiritual and absolute in things temporal.[25]

THE *LETTER* TO NORFOLK

For the next few years Newman was content to stay out of the spotlight and devote his remaining days to "sweeping up, dusting, putting [his] house in order." He sorted his letters and edited his earlier writings for republication in a uniform edition, adding critical notes to the Anglican works. Then, in October 1874, an obiter dictum in an article by the Prime Minister, William Gladstone, forced him into the fray. Reacting, no doubt, to Manning's Ultramontanist interpretation of infallibility, Gladstone allowed that "no one can become [the Roman Church's] convert without renouncing his moral and mental freedom, and placing his civil loyalty and duty at the mercy of another." This article was followed the next month by Gladstone's pamphlet *The Vatican Decrees in their bearing on Civil Allegiance*. Newman picked up his pen and for several weeks threw himself into a response which became a 150-page pamphlet in the form of *A Letter to the Duke of Norfolk* (1875), the duke being a prominent young Catholic who had attended the Oratory School. Though occasioned by the Liberal Gladstone, the *Letter* was at least equally aimed at the Ultramontanist Manning, something of a *via media* against the left and the right.[26]

Newman begins the *Letter* with some Introductory Remarks situating Gladstone's charges in the context of not only the Encyclical and *Syllabus* of 1864 and the definition of 1870 but also most immediately of the alleged Catholic pressure on the Irish Members of Parliament in 1873 for the rejection of the Irish University Bill. He then systematically addresses what he takes to be Gladstone's "main question": "Can Catholics be trustworthy subjects of the State?", beginning with sections on The Ancient Church, The Papal Church, and Divided Allegiance, and ending with sections on The Encyclical of 1864, The Syllabus, The Vatican Council, The Vatican Definition, and a Conclusion. The essence of his Conclusion is that Gladstone's charges have no grounds in that the pope's "prerogative of infallibility lies in matters speculative, and his prerogative of authority is no infallibility in laws, commands, or measures. His infallibility bears upon the domain of thought, not directly of action, and while it may fairly exercise the theologian, philosopher, or man of science, it scarcely concerns the politician." The Vatican definition did not increase the pope's authority; it simply declared the authority (and corresponding rule of obedience) that he "for centuries upon centuries had and used." Throughout his entire discussion Newman insists that dogmas, including the definition of infallibility, must be interpreted by theologians, just as civil laws are interpreted by courts. Even infallible teaching about faith and morals, whether affirming truths or condemning errors, have concrete contexts and implications in specific applications, and are thus subject to such standard principles of interpretation as legitimate minimization.[27]

Between the first and second halves of the *Letter* Newman places a pivotal section addressing its fundamental question: the relation of an individual's conscience to church authority. Because Gladstone had posed his question in terms of an English Catholic's obedience to queen or pope, Newman prefaces his position on conscience with a statement of "double allegiance" to both queen and pope. But, since "there is no rule in this world without exceptions," he gives "absolute obedience to neither." And should these allegiances ever conflict, he would decide the particular case on its own merits, after extensive consultation, by his own judgment and conscience. He sharply distinguishes such reliance on private judgment of conscience "in very extraordinary and rare, nay, impossible emergencies" from "the Protestant doctrine that Private Judgment is our *ordinary* guide in religious matters."[28]

Newman grants "that there are extreme cases [Pope and Anti-popes claiming allegiance, for example] in which Conscience may come into collision with the word of a Pope, and is to be followed in spite of that word." How is this "supreme authority of Conscience" to be explained?[29]

First, Newman asserts that the Supreme Being has an ethical character, with the "attributes of justice, truth, wisdom, sanctity, benevolence and mercy, as eternal characteristics in His nature, the very Law of His being, identical with Himself ... ." As "Creator, He implanted this Law, which is Himself, in the intelligence of all His rational creatures." This Divine Law "is the rule of ethical truth, the standard of right and wrong, a sovereign, irreversible, absolute authority in the presence of men and Angels." Implanted in humans, this eternal, Divine Law is the natural moral law. As "apprehended in the minds of individual men," this law is called conscience, and has the "prerogative of commanding obedience."[30]

Although conscience is recognized as the "voice of God" by Protestants as well as Catholics, Newman sees it reduced by others to nothing more than a "creation of man," to merely the "right of self-will." And it is this truncated and distorted meaning of conscience (a false "liberty of conscience"), Newman argues, that nineteenth-century popes have attacked in defense of the true meaning of conscience, which is, indeed, the very foundation of papal authority in theory and power in fact, the raison d'être of the papal mission.[31]

Having argued for this "high sense" of conscience "as a dutiful obedience to what claims to be a divine voice, speaking within us," Newman makes his case, against Gladstone, that "conscience cannot come into direct collision with the Church's or the Pope's infallibility ... ." First, following Aquinas, he asserts that conscience is a practical judgment for action. But, second, a pope is infallible in his assertions of general propositions or condemnations of errors, not "in his laws, nor in his commands, nor in his acts of state, nor in his administration, nor in his public policy." Thus, since "the Pope is not infallible in that subject-matter [of particular actions] in which conscience is of supreme authority," Newman concludes, "no dead-lock ... can take place between conscience and the Pope." Newman adds that when conscience has "the right of opposing the supreme, though not infallible Authority of the Pope," it also has the burden of proof, and this proof for an exceptional over-riding of the presumption of obedience must be established through serious reflection, prayer, and consultation.[32]

Though Newman ends by explicitly challenging Gladstone to move beyond vague terms and sloppy generalities and to respond to his own argument in specific details and precise words, his final assertion of "the duty of obeying our conscience at all hazards" and his famous remark about drinking to "Conscience first, and to the Pope afterwards," may be interpreted as implicit jabs at Manning's Ultramontanism.[33]

2. CONSCIENCE IN THREE DIMENSIONS

Although the *Norfolk Letter* is Newman's most famous statement on conscience, it is not alone. Indeed, the topic of conscience spans his whole adult life, from early sermons to the mature *Grammar of Assent*. In the *Letter*, where, as we have noted, the central issue is the relationship between individual conscience and church authority, Newman's focus is on conscience as a God-given practical judgment for action. Conscience as judgment is one key aspect of Newman's understanding of conscience, to be sure. But it is only one aspect of what is for Newman a multi-faceted reality. Although he did not present a systematic, comprehensive view, we may, for the sake of clarity, specify three fundamental dimensions of conscience as understood by Newman.[34] First, in the spirit of Augustine, there is conscience as *desire*. Second, following Aristotle on *phronesis*, there is conscience as *discernment*, leading to practical judgment. Third, with Aquinas, there is conscience as *demand* for decision to act in accord with judgment.

DESIRE

With Augustine, Newman believed that our hearts are restless until they rest in God. Our deepest desire, the weight of our longing, is ultimately for God, who is truth, goodness, love. "In every one of us there is naturally a void, a restlessness, a hunger of the soul, a craving after some unknown and vague happiness, which we suppose seated in wealth, fame, knowledge, in fact any worldly good which we are not ourselves possessed of … ." In Newman's view, conscience is "leading the mind to God." The "very existence" of conscience "throws us out of ourselves, and beyond ourselves, to go and seek for Him in the height and depth, whose Voice it is." Obedience "to our conscience, in all things, great and small," he says, "is the way to know the Truth." Conscience is the "echo of God's voice." In an 1837 Trinity Sunday sermon titled "Faith without Demonstration," he exhorts, "Let us aim at, let us reach after and (as it were) catch at the things of the next world. There is a voice within us, which assures us that there is something higher than earth. We cannot analyze, define, contemplate what it is that thus whispers to us. It has no shape or material form. There is that in our hearts which prompts us to religion, and which condemns and chastises sin. And," he continues, "this yearning of our nature is met and sustained, it finds an object to rest upon, when it hears of the existence of an All-powerful, All-gracious Creator. It incites us to a noble faith in what we cannot see."[35]

Conscience as desire is the source of our trustworthy, truthful notions. They are such, for Newman, because they "come from God": "I mean our certainty that there is a right and a wrong, that some things ought to be done, and other things not done; that we have duties, the neglect of which brings remorse; and further," he adds, "that God is good, wise, powerful, and righteous, and that we should try to obey Him. All these notions, and a multitude of others like these, come by natural conscience, i.e. they are impressed on all our minds from our earliest years without our trouble. They do not proceed from the mere exercise of our minds," he insists, "though it is true they are strengthened and formed thereby. They proceed from God, whether within us or without us ... ."[36]

Conscience is desire for the fullness of God because of God's presence within us. For Newman, "a true Christian ... may almost be defined as one who has a ruling sense of God's presence within him"—a presence "not externally, not in nature merely, or in providence, but in his innermost heart, or in his *conscience*. A man is justified whose conscience is illuminated by God, so that he habitually realizes that all his thoughts, all the first springs of his moral life, all his motives and his wishes, are open to Almighty God." Newman acknowledges that "absolute certainty about our state cannot be attained at all in this life; but the nearest approach to such certainty which is possible," he says, "would seem to be afforded by this consciousness of openness and singleness of mind, this good understanding ... between the soul and its conscience." On this he turns to St. Paul: "Our rejoicing is this, the testimony of our conscience, that in simplicity and godly sincerity, ... we have had our conversation in the world" (2 Cor 1: 12).[37]

Newman assumes "the presence of God in our conscience ... ," where God "lives as a Personal, All-seeing, All-judging Being ... ." This presence, this luminous immediacy of God in the innermost being of a person, in one's conscience, is the source of natural law and grounds the possibility of knowing God. In this sense, conscience is "more than a man's own self." This is all nicely summarized by the title character in Newman's novel *Callista*: "I feel … God within my heart. I feel myself in his presence. He says to me, 'Do this: don't do that.' You may tell me that this dictate is a mere law of my nature, as is to joy or to grieve. I cannot understand this. No," she continues, "it is the echo of a person speaking to me. Nothing shall persuade me that it does not ultimately proceed from a person external to me. It carries with it its proof of its divine origin. My nature feels towards it as towards a person. When I obey it, I feel a satisfaction; when I disobey, a soreness—just like that which I feel in pleasing or offending some revered friend."[38] But this dictate needs to be specified concretely by each person for every particular time and place. And this requires discernment.

DISCERNMENT

If conscience as desire is most radically a search for truth, and ultimately for God who is truth, conscience as discernment is a search for the truth of what should be done here and now in *this* particular concrete situation of value.

In the course of discussing the existence of God in the *Grammar*, Newman asserts as a first, foundational principle "that we have by nature a conscience." "I assume," he says, "that conscience has a legitimate place among our mental acts; as really so, as the action of memory, of reasoning, of imagination, or as the sense of the beautiful;" further, he assumes, "that, as there are objects which, when presented to the mind, cause it to feel grief, regret, joy, or desire, so there are things which excite in us approbation or blame, and which we in consequence call right or wrong; and which, experienced in ourselves, kindle in us that specific sense of pleasure or pain, which goes by the name of a good or bad conscience." Taking this much for granted, Newman will go on "to show that in this special feeling, which follows on the commission of what we call right or wrong, lie the materials for the real apprehension of a Divine Sovereign and Judge."[39]

At this point, however, Newman makes a basic distinction in his understanding of conscience. "The feeling of conscience being," he repeats, "a certain keen sensibility, pleasant or painful,—self-approval and hope, or compunction and fear,—attendant on certain of our actions, which in consequence we call right or wrong, is twofold:—it is a moral sense, and a sense of duty; a judgment of the reason and a magisterial dictate." Thus, Newman concludes, "conscience has both a critical and a judicial office, and though its promptings, in the breasts of the millions of human beings to whom it is given, are not in all cases correct, that does not necessarily interfere with the force of its testimony and of its sanction: its testimony that there is a right and a wrong, and its sanction to that testimony conveyed in the feelings which attend on right or wrong conduct."[40] So, conscience is both a moral judgment and a dictate of duty. Its act is indivisible, but with two distinct aspects. Here we can focus on the first aspect, moral judgment and the process of discernment leading to it.

Conscience, Newman writes, "is a personal guide, and I use it because I must use myself; I am as little able to think by any mind but my own as to breathe with another's lungs." Conscience, he continues, "is nearer to me than any other means of knowledge." In characterizing conscience, then, Newman insists on referring to his own self, to his own mind—the mind, which, in discussing the central control of the Illative Sense, he calls "the living mind."[41]

If for Newman the Illative Sense is the living mind reasoning across the whole range of concrete, particular reality, conscience as discernment is the living mind reasoning specifically about the concrete particulars of moral value and duty. Conscience as discernment, to put it another way, is the Illative Sense operating in its moral mode. And his model of this implicit, non-discursive, imaginative moral reasoning is Aristotle's *phronesis*, the "directing, controlling, and determining principle" in matters personal and social. "What it is to be virtuous," he writes, "how we are to gain the just idea and standard of virtue, how we are to approximate in practice to our own standard, what is right and wrong in a particular case, for the answers in fulness and accuracy to these and similar questions, the philosopher refers us to no code of laws, to no moral treatise, because no science of life, applicable to the case of an individual, has been or can be written."[42]

Newman goes on to endorse this Aristotelian view as "undoubtedly true," and asserts that "an ethical system," the product of explicit, discursive reason, "may supply laws, general rules, guiding principles, a number of examples, suggestions, landmarks, limitations, cautions, distinctions, solutions of critical or anxious difficulties; but who," he asks, "is to apply them to a particular case? whither can we go, except to the living intellect, our own, or another's? What is written," he says,

THE ROMAN CATHOLIC NEWMAN & CONSCIENCE

"is too vague, too negative for our need. It bids us avoid extremes; but it cannot ascertain for us, according to our present need, the golden mean. The authoritative oracle, which is to decide our path," he continues, "is something more searching and manifold than such jejune generalizations as treatises can give, which are most distinct and clear when we least need them." This oracle, rather, "is seated in the mind of the individual, who is thus his own law, his own teacher, and his own judge in those special cases of duty which are personal to him." This oracle, Newman explains, "comes of an acquired habit, though it has its first origins in nature itself, and is formed and matured by practice and experience; and it manifests itself, not in any breadth of view, any philosophical comprehension of the mutual relations of duty towards duty, or any consistency in its teachings, but it is a capacity sufficient for the occasion, deciding what ought to be done here and now, by this given person, under these given circumstances." Again, focusing on the first-person, actual here and now, Newman stresses that this oracle of conscience "decides nothing hypothetical, it does not determine what a man should do ten years hence, or what another should do at this time. It may indeed happen to decide ten years hence as it does now, and to decide a second case now as it now decides a first; still its present act is for the present, not for the distant or the future."[43]

Newman further emphasizes the personal and concrete nature of conscience in his assertion that "the rule of conduct for one man is not always the rule for another, though the rule is always one and the same in the abstract … . To learn his own duty in his own case, each individual must have recourse to his own rule; … not to the dead letter of a treatise or a code. A living, present authority, himself or another, is his immediate guide in matters of a personal, social, or political character… . [E]very one of his acts, to be praiseworthy, must be in accordance with this practical sense. Thus it is," Newman concludes, "and not by science, that he perfects the virtues of justice, self-command, magnanimity, generosity, gentleness, and all others. *Phronesis* is the regulating principle of every one of them."[44]

Judgments of *phronesis*, of the Illative Sense focused on moral issues of value and duty, are the most obvious instances of what Newman means by certainty. As early as 1830 he had argued that "*Certainty* in the business of life means *a conviction sufficient for practice*," a conviction rooted in "evidence from probabilities." In his view, "every thing we do, is done on probabilities… . No facts are known, no practical matters conducted, on demonstrative proof, which is found in pure mathematics alone and subjects of a similar nature ... ." The living mind of an experienced and virtuous person, of one who knows life as a master knows a particular field, is the only criterion of "evidence from probabilities" for "a certainty sufficient for action ... ."[45] "We judge for ourselves, by our own lights, and on our own principles; and the criterion of truth," Newman asserts, "is not so much the manipulation of propositions, as the intellectual and moral character of the person maintaining them ... ."[46] *Phronesis* is not infallible, but for Newman "there is no inherent weakness in an argument from probabilities in a question of practice."[47] Perhaps one of Newman's famous images makes his point most clearly. "The best illustration ... is that of a cable, which is made up of a number of separate threads, each feeble, yet together as sufficient as an iron rod," Newman wrote in an 1864 letter. "An iron rod represents mathematical or strict demonstration; a cable represents moral demonstration, which is an assemblage of probabilities, separately insufficient for certainty, but, when put together, irrefragable."[48]

Clearly, then, for Newman, conscience as discernment, rooted in experience and virtue, is primarily a first-person, imaginative, implicit, non-discursive mode of moral reasoning focused practically on particular, concrete situations of value and duty: *what should I do here and now?* It is distinct from, but positively related to, abstract, analytical modes of reasoning, which it employs when appropriate. This holistic, affective, historical discernment process produces the practical judgments for action Newman highlights in his *Letter* to Norfolk. Though beyond the legitimate range of church authority, discerning conscience constitutes something of a *via media* between reliance on abstract (often absolute) moral principles on the one hand and surrender to a lawless situationism on the other. It brings the search for truth effectively to the world of action. But its practical guidance does not come without a price. Embedded within the practical judgment of conscience, unlike other judgments, is a demand, what Newman calls a magisterial "dictate" of duty, a demand that we decide to act in accord with our judgment, that we follow our conscience. To that demand, that magisterial dictate, we now turn.

DEMAND

Although Newman's most famous statement on conscience in his Norfolk *Letter* focused on conscience as discernment leading to practical judgment, his most fundamentally strategic consideration of conscience in the *Grammar* (and earlier works) featured the dictate or demand dimension of conscience as the basis for assenting to God's existence.[49]

In the *Grammar's* section on "Belief in One God," Newman announces his focus on conscience "simply as the dictate of an authoritative monitor bearing upon the details of conduct as they come before us ... ." Here he intends to "consider conscience, not as a rule of right conduct, but as a sanction of right conduct," which he holds as "its primary and most authoritative aspect," and the "ordinary sense of the word. Half the world," he says, "would be puzzled to know what was meant by the moral sense; but every one knows what is meant by a good or bad conscience." It is in this sense that "conscience is ever forcing on us by threats and by promises that we must follow the right and avoid the wrong ... ." Indeed conscience, as noted above, is "more than a man's own self." As Newman explains, "The man himself has not power over it, or only with extreme difficulty; he did not make it, he cannot destroy it. He may silence it in particular cases or directions, he may distort its enunciations, but he cannot, or it is quite the exception if he can, he cannot emancipate himself from it. He can disobey it, he may refuse to use it; but it remains."[50]

As magisterial dictate, Newman claims, conscience is "one and the same in the mind of every one, whatever be its particular errors in particular minds as to the acts which it orders to be done or to be avoided ... ." And, he continues, "in this respect it corresponds to our perception of the beautiful and deformed. As we have naturally a sense of the beautiful and graceful in nature and art, though tastes proverbially differ, so we have a sense of duty and obligation, whether we all associate it with the same certain actions in particular or not." At this point, however, "Taste and Conscience part company: for the sense of beautifulness, as indeed the Moral Sense, has no special relations to persons, but contemplates objects in themselves ... ." In contrast, Newman asserts, conscience "is concerned with persons primarily, and with actions mainly as viewed in their doers, or rather with self alone and one's own actions, and with others only indirectly and as if in association with self."[51]

Further, and here Newman hints at his theological argument, while "taste is its own evidence, appealing to nothing beyond its own sense of the beautiful or the ugly, ... conscience does not repose on itself, but vaguely reaches forward to something beyond itself, and dimly discerns a sanction higher than itself for its decisions, as is evidenced in that keen sense of obligation and responsibility which informs them." Thus, Newman continues, "we are accustomed to speak of conscience as a voice, a term which we should never think of applying to the sense of the beautiful; and moreover a voice, or the echo of a voice, imperative and constraining, like no other dictate in the whole of our experience." And, he goes on, "in consequence of this prerogative of dictating and commanding, which is of its essence, Conscience has an intimate bearing on our affections and emotions, leading us to reverence and awe, hope and fear, especially fear, a feeling which is foreign for the most part, not only to Taste, but even to the Moral Sense ... ."[52]

Anyone who has fallen into immorality, Newman states, "has a lively sense of responsibility and guilt, though the act be no offense against society,—of distress and apprehension, even though it may be of present service to him,—of compunction and regret, though in itself it be most pleasurable,—of confusion of face, though it may have no witnesses." He goes on to explain that "these various perturbations of mind which are characteristic of a bad conscience, and may be very considerable,—self-reproach, poignant shame, haunting remorse, chill dismay at the prospect of the future,—and their contraries, when the conscience is good, as real though less forcible, self-approval, inward peace, lightness of heart, and the like,—these emotions constitute a specific difference," he says, "between conscience and our other intellectual senses, ... as indeed they would also constitute between conscience and the moral sense, supposing these two were not aspects of one and the same feeling, exercised upon one and the same subject-matter."[53]

From this focus on emotions Newman goes on to make his key theological point. He insists that conscience, unlike the sense of the beautiful or even the moral sense, is "always emotional." For him, therefore, it is no wonder that conscience "always involves the recognition of a living object, towards which it is directed." Affections, he says, are "correlative with persons." Making a comparison to the feelings of a child toward parents, he argues that "If, as is the case, we feel responsibility, are ashamed, are frightened, at transgressing the voice of conscience, this implies that there is One [intelligent being] to whom we are responsible, before whom we are ashamed, whose claims upon us we fear." Conscience, he continues, "excites all these painful emotions, confusion, foreboding, self-condemnation; and on the other hand it sheds upon us a deep peace, a sense of security, a resignation, and a hope, which there is no sensible, no earthly object to elicit." And, he concludes, "If the cause of these emotions does not belong to this visible world," their Object "must be Supernatural and Divine; and thus the phenomena of Conscience, as a dictate, avail to impress the imagination with a picture of a Supreme Governor, a Judge, holy, just, powerful, all-seeing, retributive, and is the creative principle of religion, as the Moral Sense is the principle of ethics." After drawing out some of the implications of this fundamental point, Newman sums up: "To a mind ... carefully formed upon the basis of its natural conscience, the world, both of nature and of man, does but give back a reflection of those truths about the One Living God, which have been familiar to it from childhood.... Thus conscience is a connecting principle between the creature and his Creator ... ."[54]

Newman's argument for God's existence from conscience *as dictate* may have a ring of the superego to a contemporary ear, and he may have fared better for the ages with an argument from conscience *as desire*, but his basic point about the unique nature of conscience remains: judgments of conscience, unlike other judgments, include an intrinsic commanding dictate, an imperative demand for consistent action. His insistence that conscience is more than self-consistency notwithstanding,[55] the critical point holds: judgments of conscience demand to be followed. Interpretation of this demand is another matter.

3. CONCLUSION

Newman's analysis of conscience is powerful and nuanced, with the desire, discernment, and demand dimensions duly specified at various points. But he did not explicitly bring all three dimensions together into one integrated understanding of conscience as *the* fundamental cognitive-moral-affective-religious reality of the self reaching beyond itself.

Newman had a grand view of conscience, but he did not spell out the intrinsic relationships among the three foundational elements of conscience he had discovered in Augustine, Aristotle, and Aquinas. He did not detail (and here I feebly attempt to echo his characteristic serial style) how desire, discernment, and demand are interlinked, unfolding facets of a single dynamic reality; how the cognitively, morally, affectively, and religiously conscious person, the existential self, *is* conscience; how the self is at root a divinely inspired and targeted *desire* for transcendence, for reaching out to the reality of the other in all its forms, ultimately to the Other in which it finds its true self; how in the turmoil of daily life this desiring self struggles to *discern* what he or she should do in a particular, concrete situation of value; and how this self's practical judgment *demands* to be followed, with disobedience resulting not in some external punishment but in a violation of one's very self, of one's desire, one's divine calling, to transcendence. In other, first-person singular words, we can briefly identify Newman's three dimensions of conscience with self in this way: I *am* conscience in my radical *desire* for self-transcendence; I *am* conscience when I realize this desire by striving to *discern* how I should act here and now; I *am* conscience when I experience the *demand* to follow my best judgment and respond to it. Identifying conscience with self in this way clarifies—in the face of every temptation to reify it—that conscience is not any kind of thing (faculty, voice, heart, etc., as appealing as some metaphors can be), but that it is simply the fundamental mode of being human. Newman laid out the major themes of his great Symphony in D Major, the "Conscientia"; their arrangement he left to others.[56]

All this is to say that Newman did not articulate intellectually in a systematic way what in practice he managed to realize in his own life: a *unified* conscience as a radical dynamism for truth, goodness, and love, ineluctably impelling him to the ultimate reality of truth, goodness, love itself, to God. As we saw in earlier chapters, for Newman conscience was not only an academic concern or, as he might say, a notion in his mind, but a real drive in his life that had led him at age fifteen to a deeply personal Evangelical faith through a basic Christian moral conversion, then in his later twenties to Anglo-Catholicism through a structural cognitive conversion, and finally at mid-life forced him through a difficult course of discernment and an excruciating process of deliberation to his decision to convert, to move from Oxford to Rome, where, of course, he found yet more grist for the mill of his ever restless conscience.

EPILOGUE

Two honorific events, one in each of the two worlds Newman had inhabited as Anglican and Roman, fittingly marked his eighth decade. Together they brought a symbolic unity to a life that had seemed forever divided.

In February 1878 Newman traveled to Oxford to formally accept an invitation to become Trinity College's first honorary Fellow. This honor culminated the rehabilitation of Newman's reputation at his former university, a "change of feeling" that had begun in England generally with the appearance of his *Apologia*.[1] He had always been devoted to Trinity since his undergraduate days, and it was in the *Apologia* that he had written lovingly of his first college "which was so dear to me, and which held on its foundation so many who had been so kind to me both when I was a boy, and all through my Oxford life. Trinity had never been unkind to me." And he had continued in his characteristic imagery: "There used to be much snap-dragon growing on the walls opposite my freshman's rooms there, and I had for years taken it as an emblem of my own perpetual residence even unto my death in my University."[2] Nothing could have meant more to him than this honorary Fellowship, retrieving as it did the half of his life he had had to abandon—except possibly one other thing.

The following year, in May 1879, a little more than a year after the death of Pius IX, and only four years after the Norfolk *Letter's* toast to conscience, Newman was elevated to the College of Cardinals by the new Pope Leo XIII. Newman's speech for the occasion interprets the honor as a vindication of his liberal Catholicism, but also distinguishes that liberalism from religious Liberalism, "the doctrine that there is no positive truth in religion," which he once more denounces as a "great mischief," an "error overspreading, as a snare, the whole earth ... ."[3] For the coat of arms of his cardinalate he chose from St. Francis de Sales the motto "cor ad cor loquitur." His loyalty and service to the Roman Catholic Church thus recognized, the meaning of the second half of his life was now also secured for posterity. He was now John Henry Cardinal Newman, Fellow of Trinity College (*Oxon.*), honored publicly in two worlds he had never really felt fully at home in privately.

As the years of his ninth decade passed, Newman's physical strength steadily declined; but not his mental powers. Finally, on August 10, 1890, he fell ill, and died of pneumonia the next day. As he had requested, he was buried a week later at Rednal in the grave of his great friend Ambrose St. John, with the inscription "Ex umbris et imaginibus in veritatem." In 1894 a Newman Club was established at the University of Pennsylvania, the first of numerous Catholic centers of study and worship named in his honor at secular colleges and universities. (In 1888 the Catholic Club at Oxford University had been renamed the Newman Society.) In 1991 the Roman Catholic Church declared John Henry Cardinal Newman "Venerable." The Vatican has given approval for his beatification in 2010.

APPENDIX

My analysis of Newman presumes much of my earlier theoretical work on conscience, conversion, development, self, and self-transcendence, especially in my book *Christian Conversion*. While the present volume includes many specific aspects of that work, the edited material reproduced in this appendix offers background that should be helpful for placing Newman's experience into a larger theoretical context.

SELF

My theoretical premise is that the fundamental desire of the self is to transcend itself in relationship: to the world, to others, to God. But only a developed, powerful self has the strength to realize significant transcendence. My approach, therefore, is elliptical; it recognizes two focal points in the fundamental human desire: the drive *to be a self*, a center of strength; and the dynamism *to move beyond the self* in relationship. My interpretation of the desiring self not only includes both elements, it insists on their inextricable connection; the desires to be a self and to reach out beyond the self must always be understood together: separation *and* attachment, independence *and* belonging, autonomy *and* relationship. The self exists only in relationship to the other. This dual desire of the human heart is expressed in the two words of my basic theoretical term, "self-transcendence."

More fully, my model of the self is that of a double ellipse, of an ellipse within an ellipse; for the dual desire for self-transcendence exists at the subject-pole of a dipolar self. Briefly, the self (the person precisely as conscious) is a unity-in-tension—a dynamic, dipolar, dialectical, embodied, first-person reality constituted by consciousness and experienced as "I" (a creating-self at the subject-pole striving for meaning and value in self-transcending relationships) and as "me" (a created-self at the object-pole consisting of material, social, and spiritual selves; morally, one's character).

SELF-TRANSCENDENCE

Self-transcendence, as delineated by Bernard Lonergan, occurs in our effective response to the radical drive, the dynamic exigence of the human spirit for meaning, truth, value, and love. Though single in source and ultimate goal, this questioning drive of the human spirit manifests itself in multiple, interconnected questions: the drive for understanding seeks meaning in questions for intelligence; but not any meaning, for once attained, meaning is critically scrutinized by the drive for truth in questions for reflection heading toward realistic judgment. And when understanding and judgment are within a practical pattern oriented toward action, there follows the further moral question for deliberation: given my judgment of the situation and required action, what am I going to *do* about it? Finally, this practical questioning oriented toward action occurs within—and is permeated by—a matrix of affectivity which must be strong enough to support the required action over the obstacles of conflicting interests. What, in the last analysis, am I going to commit myself to in love?

In this view, every achievement of creative understanding, realistic judgment, responsible choice, and genuine love is an instance of self-transcendence. Among all the possible realizations of human potential, such cognitive, moral, and affective self-transcendence is the criterion of authentic self-realization. The Gospel demand calling us to intelligent, responsible, loving service of our neighbor requires no more and no less than the fulfillment of this fundamental personal drive for self-transcendence. As the criterion of personal authenticity, self-transcending love is also the norm by which every other personal concern, interest, need, desire or wish must be judged—and, if necessary, sacrificed. Fidelity to this law of the human spirit, this radical dynamism for self-transcending love, sums up the demand of the Christian life because it is a response to the divine within us—God's gift of love.

In contrast to interpretations of conscience embedded in essentially compartmentalized or reductionistic views, an approach to conscience deep and comprehensive enough to allow a full understanding of conversion must be developed within a holistic and emergent interpretation of the personal subject; in short, within a theory of self-transcendence. Indeed, conscience must be understood, not only as the morally conscious self or as a fundamental mode of self-awareness, but precisely as the dynamic core of conscious subjectivity which constitutes the very being of the person, driving him or her toward the authenticity of self-transcendence. Conscience and conversion, then, can be most adequately understood as intrinsically connected in a normative theory of self-transcendence.

The concept of self-transcendence can be helpful in clarifying the difficult realities of self-love, neighbor-love, and God-love, and their inter-relationships.

The distinction between healthy self-love and destructive selfishness lies precisely in self-transcendence, in the distinction between self-as-subject and self-as-object. We love ourselves in an authentic way by loving others. Loving others is loving ourselves because acting for the true good of others (their growth, happiness) is acting for our own true good (realization of our capacity for self-transcendence). This is loving ourselves-as-subjects in the act of loving others. To love ourselves as we love our neighbors is, as the Gospel puts it, to love our neighbors as ourselves. In contrast, selfishness is the inappropriate attempt to love ourselves-as-objects, to fulfill our every want and wish. The self the Gospel calls us to renounce is the false self—the egocentric self-interests that obstruct the self-transcending love of others and ourselves that we are called to. We renounce the false self in order to love the true self-as-subject in and through its very reaching out to love others. Like consciousness, in which the self is known as subject in the same act that knows objects, authentic self-love is not a reflexive, second act of loving self-as-object, but an interior dimension (subject) of the one act of loving another (object). Attempting to love the self in any other way (as object) is certain to fail, is doomed to selfishness. Like happiness, self-love is elusive: the more we seek it, the more it escapes us. Both happiness and self-love are realized only in self-transcending love of others. And truly loving others is also, of course, loving God. An adequate understanding of self-transcendence, then, reveals the radical identity of these loves—to love our neighbors is simultaneously to love ourselves and our God.

CONVERSION AND DEVELOPMENT

In our analysis of Newman's first conversion in chapter one, reference was made to the eight crises of Erik Erikson's life cycle. Here, a somewhat expanded consideration of Erikson's last four crises—then complemented by key stages of structural development—will further detail some relationships between development and conversion.

First, Erikson's psychosocial interpretation of the *identity* crisis in terms of a commitment of fidelity to value specifies an intrinsically moral dimension in adolescent conversion. Second, the psychosocial crisis of *intimacy* in the young adult raises the question of a further conversion—of the possibility, even normative necessity, of the person, now secure in his or her own identity, risking that identity by falling in love. Third, Erikson's specification—at the adult crisis of *generativity*—of a fully ethical orientation of care and responsibility in contrast to the ideological orientation to value of adolescence points to a properly adult moral conversion beyond the possibilities of youth. Finally, Erikson's identification of a crisis of *integrity* vs. despair in the older adult suggests that the years after mid-life might be the occasion for a transformation of life radical enough to truly be called religious.

Taking these four psychosocial clues from the crises of Erikson's life cycle, we have the possibility of the following fundamental conversions: (1) moral conversion; (2) affective conversion; (3) cognitive or critical moral conversion; (4) religious conversion. Each of these conversions may occur in an explicitly religious context, but such a context is not necessary. When they occur in a Christian context, they are dimensions of a full Christian conversion.

Conversion is commonly understood as a change in the *content* of a person's faith or fundamental orientation. Thus, for example, a person in becoming a Christian adopts the Christian story as an orientation to life—or drops it for another master story in converting from Christianity to something else. If we say that a person's fundamental horizon is established by a set of existential questions, conversion as a change of content may be understood as *horizontal* conversion: new answers (content) to old questions within an established horizon.

As valuable as this content approach to conversion is—and Newman's move from the Anglican Church to the Roman is a prime example—my principal focus here is on a complementary approach suggested by structural theories of development, especially those of Piaget, Kohlberg, Fowler, and Kegan. In this approach, conversion is viewed from the perspective of *structure* rather than content, and may be understood as a *vertical* conversion: radically new questions creatively restructuring content (old or new) into a totally new horizon.

MORAL CONVERSION

Lawrence Kohlberg is widely known for his six stages of moral reasoning development, which he divides into pairs on three levels: preconventional, conventional, and postconventional. Kohlberg gives no attention to conversion, but careful reflection on the nature of structural stages indicates that stage transition (especially between major levels) is a form of conversion. Here I will concentrate on the transition from preconventional to conventional moral reasoning. Kohlberg claims that this transition occurs, at the earliest, in the young adolescent, occasioned in part by the emergence of Piagetian formal cognitive operations.

Fundamentally this transition is a shift from a premoral to a moral orientation, that is, from a radically egocentric orientation in which the criterion for judgment is self-interested satisfaction to a social orientation in which the criterion for judgment is value (in various conventionally defined forms). The actual realization of value in one's life is a further issue, but this new criterion—rooted in the ability to distinguish the valuable from the valuable-for-me—establishes a new horizon, sets a new personal agenda. Content will vary greatly among individuals, but morally converted horizons are similar inasmuch as concern for value is their defining and constitutive character. When structural and psychosocial stages coincide, moral conversion to value meshes perfectly with the adolescent's discovery of self in fidelity.

AFFECTIVE CONVERSION

Moral conversion to value calls us beyond ourselves; it is more of a challenge than an achievement; it discloses the gap between the self that we are and the self we should be. The challenge to close that gap is the challenge to move beyond ourselves not only in our knowing but also in our deciding and our acting, the challenge to make our action consistent with our judgment of what we should do and be. But we meet that challenge, we close that gap, we really move beyond ourselves with regularity, insofar as—and only insofar as—we fall in love. For only in such falling-in-love do our full persons escape the centripetal force of our persistent egocentric gravity. Then we become beings-in-love, existential principles of responsible action consistent with our best judgment.

For many years Kohlberg's cognitive-structural perspective never particularly focused on affectivity or moral action. In his later years, however, the question of distinctively adult moral development prompted Kohlberg to look to Erikson's existential crises and psychosocial ego-strengths or virtues with renewed interest. In the next section we shall see how Kohlberg came to link postconventional moral development with the generativity of Erikson's adult ethical orientation, characterized by care and responsibility. Here I simply want to emphasize how the young adult's prior Eriksonian crisis of intimacy—with its defining strength of love—may be the occasion of an affective conversion, a fundamental relocation of the self's dynamic center of gravity. That Kohlberg did not give any special attention to the crisis of intimacy must be seen as an important oversight insofar as the structural decentering of the self in affective conversion is a necessary condition for the care and responsibility of the ethical adult's generativity.

Robert Kegan's analysis of the emergence at Stage 5 of a self capable of sharing itself while remaining distinct offers a structural interpretation of affective conversion critically grounded in the key distinction between pre-identity fusion and post-identity intimacy.

COGNITIVE OR CRITICAL MORAL CONVERSION

For more than half a century Jean Piaget traced the course of cognitive development from the infant's sensorimotor activity, through the acquisition of language and symbolic functions in early childhood and the emergence of concrete operational thought in later childhood, to the appearance of formal operations in adolescence. Each transition to a higher stage introduces a significant new element. Concrete operations systematize previously acquired cognitive activities. Formal operations give wings to operational thinking, freeing it from the here and now limitations of concrete experience. When it occurs, such liberation from the concrete inevitably becomes escape from the real, as the formal thinking of the idealistic adolescent revels in its new power of flight. Only the vocational experiences proper to the adult bring the winged perspective back to earth, integrating formal thought's universalizing abstraction with the empirical dimension of concrete operations into the power of realistic judgment.

While such development is obviously fundamental to one's understanding of the world, it is also crucial for self-understanding. For insofar as a person who has developed through concrete and formal operations to adult realistic judgment can reflect this power back on the self, precisely as a knower, there is beyond cognitive development also the possibility of cognitive conversion: the critical recognition of the constitutive and normative role of one's own judgment in knowing reality and therefore value. A person who experiences such critical understanding of the self as knower ceases to look beyond the self somewhere "out there" for a criterion of the real or the valuable. For cognitive conversion consists precisely in discovering that criterion in one's own realistic judgment.

Kohlberg's third, postconventional level of moral reasoning, as rooted in self-chosen, universal principles, requires exactly this kind of cognitive conversion in the moral dimension, i.e., critical moral conversion. Basic moral conversion to conventional morality is essentially uncritical, locating authority in absolutely *given* social values. To become postconventional, one must discover the final criterion of value in one's own critical judgment, and thereby become the author of one's own moral life. Critical moral conversion to a postconventional stance goes beyond restructuring one's horizon in terms of value, then, by grounding that horizon of value in the reality of oneself as a critical, originating value. Kohlberg believes that, in addition to advanced cognitive development, postconventional moral transformation requires existential adult experiences of irreversible life decisions and of care and responsibility for others.

RELIGIOUS CONVERSION

James Fowler's analysis of faith development presupposes—in its distinction between Stage 3 Synthetic-Conventional Faith and Stage 4 Individuative-Reflective Faith—the same kind of cognitive conversion to a critical standpoint of being one's own authority. Fowler's analysis reaches beyond this critical stance, however, to a postcritical Stage 6 Universalizing Faith, whose felt sense of ultimate environment includes all being.

Indeed, even Kohlberg, after many years of research on moral reasoning development, began—within the context of considering development in older adults—to raise the question of a seventh, religious stage. Kohlberg's point is that if a person reaches Stage 6 of moral reasoning, and seriously tries to live a life of principled justice for a number of years, that person will inevitably ask the most fundamental question of all: "Why be just in an unjust world?" or, most simply, "Why be moral?" In fact, in Kohlberg's view, only such a person can ask this question, which he regards as ultimately a religious question, in a psychologically serious way. In his speculations, Kohlberg sees a religious Stage 7 beginning in the despair of perceiving human life as finite from the perspective of the infinite—the meaninglessness of life in the face of death, for example. Continuation toward a more cosmic perspective in non-egoistic contemplative experience leads to identifying with the cosmic or infinite perspective. The structural result is a decentering figure-ground shift in which despair is overcome by the contemplative experience of cosmic unity implicit in the despair. For Kohlberg, this experience is correlative to Erikson's final psychosocial task of integrating life's meaning.

This decentering figure-ground shift, which Kohlberg says cannot be realized on purely rational grounds, is what Christian theologians mean when they refer to a religious conversion that is not just the joining of a new religious group but is the radical reorientation of one's entire life that occurs when God is allowed to move from the periphery to the center of one's being. When this radical religious conversion is seen from the perspective of total self-surrender, the relativizing of human autonomy is stressed.

Properly understood, one surrenders not oneself or one's personal moral autonomy, but one's illusion of absolute autonomy. But such total surrender is possible only for the person who has totally fallen in love with a mysterious, uncomprehended God, for the person who has been grasped by an other-worldly love and completely transformed into a being-in-love. Such religious conversion is not only rare, it is not even religious in any ordinary sense. One need not be "religious" to experience it; indeed, when it is experienced by an explicitly religious person, such radical transformation might be best understood as a conversion from religion to God.

CONVERSION OF CONSCIENCE

The above reference to content and structure highlights the point that conscience, the radical drive of the personal subject for self-transcendence, always has a particular concrete shape, a specific horizon. This concrete shape of conscience constitutes the moral quality of a subject, the "sort of person" one is; in the fullest sense of the word, it is *character.*

Conscience, then, is to be understood in terms of both structure and content. If conscience in the most radical sense is the developing *dynamism* of the person for self-transcendence, it is also *structure and content* in the sense of the specific concrete shape taken by that dynamism as it is formed by the discoveries, decisions, and deeds through which a subject creates his or her "second nature" or character as a particular "sort of person." It is in this concrete sense of conscience as character that a person's specific insights, judgments, and decisions have their source.

In fundamental conversion, then, there is both continuity and discontinuity. Conversion radically redirects and transforms the concrete shape and orientation of personal subjectivity, the structure and content of one's conscience as character; thus the discontinuity. But if conscience as character is changed in conversion, conscience as the radical drive for self-transcendence remains. Thus basic conversion, a transformation of the person's whole orientation, a radically new beginning, occurs within the continuity of the subject's fundamental dynamism for self-transcendence.

ERIKSON	PIAGET	KOHLBERG	FOWLER	KEGAN	CONVERSIONS
8) Integrity/Despair Wisdom		7) Religious	6) Universalizing		Religious
7) Generativity/ Stagnation Care		6) Universal Principles	5) Conjunctive		Critical Moral
	Contextual-Dialectic				
6) Intimacy/Isolation Love		5) Social Contract		5) Interindividual	Affective
			4) Individuative-Reflective		
		4½) Relativist			
5) Identity/Confusion Fidelity	Full Formal	4) Authority-Social order		4) Institutional	Moral
(Affiliation/ Abandonment)	Early Formal	3) Interpersonal Concordance	3) Synthetic-Conventional	3) Interpersonal	
4) Industry/Inferiority Competence	Concrete	2) Instrumental-Relativist	2) Mythic-Literal	2) Imperial	
3) Initiative/Guilt Purpose	Preoperational	1) Punishment-Obedience	1) Intuitive-Projective	1) Impulsive	
2) Autonomy/Shame, Doubt Will					
1) Trust/Mistrust Hope	Sensorimotor	0) Amoral	0) Undifferentiated	0) Incorporative	

NOTES

PREFACE

1. Jasper Newton (Jack) Daniel (c.1850-1911) established his distillery in Lynchburg, TN in 1866, two years after the publication of Newman's *Apologia pro Vita Sua* (1864). We do not know with certitude that Newman ever sipped any of Jack's Old No. 7; likewise, we cannot be sure that Jack ever dipped into Newman's *Apologia*.

2. John Henry Cardinal Newman, *An Essay on the Development of Christian Doctrine* (New York: Longmans, Green, 1949), 38.

3. See Walter E. Conn, *Christian Conversion* (New York: Paulist, 1986; reprint, Eugene, OR: Wipf & Stock, 2006).

4. Basic developmental sources include: Erik H. Erikson, *Childhood and Society*, 2nd ed. (New York: Norton, 1963) and, of course, *Young Man Luther* (New York: Norton, 1958); Jean Piaget, *Six Psychological Studies*, ed. D. Elkind, trans. A. Tenzor (New York: Random House Vintage, 1968); Lawrence Kohlberg, *The Psychology of Moral Development* (San Francisco: Harper & Row, 1984); James W. Fowler, *Stages of Faith* (San Francisco: Harper & Row, 1981); and Robert Kegan, *The Evolving Self* (Cambridge, MA: Harvard University Press, 1982). For more on development, with detailed references, see my *Christian Conversion*.

5. See Bernard Häring, *Free and Faithful in Christ*, vol. 1 (New York: Seabury, 1978); Charles E. Curran, "Conversion: The Central Moral Message of Jesus," in his *A New Look at Christian Morality* (Notre Dame, IN: Fides, 1968), 25-71; and Bernard Lonergan, *Method in Theology* (New York: Herder and Herder, 1972).

6. Among the many skeptical views of Newman, see Valerie Pitt, "Demythologising Newman," in David Nicholls and Fergus Kerr, eds., *John Henry Newman: Reason, Rhetoric and Romanticism* (Carbondale: Southern Illinois University Press, 1991), 13-27, and Valentine Cunningham, "Dangerous Conceits or Confirmations Strong?" in ibid., 233-52.

7. The key autobiographical sources are John Henry Cardinal Newman, *Apologia pro Vita Sua*, ed. C. F. Harrold (New York: Longmans, Green, 1947); hereafter *Apo.*, and *John Henry Newman: Autobiographical Writings*, ed. H. Tristram (New York: Sheed and Ward, 1956); hereafter *AW*. The 1874 Memoir in *AW* is written in the third person. The standard edition of Newman's correspondence and diaries is *The Letters and Diaries of John Henry Newman*, ed. C. S. Dessain *et al.* (vols. 1-8, Oxford: Clarendon, 1978-99; vols. 9-10, New York: Oxford University Press, 2006; vols. 11-22, London: Nelson, 1961-72; vols. 23-31, Oxford: Clarendon, 1973-77; vol. 32, Oxford: Oxford University Press, 2008); hereafter *LD*. The

uniform edition of Newman's works is available online in full text at *www. newmanreader.org.*

8. Among the many volumes on Newman's life, see Vincent Ferrer Blehl, *Pilgrim Journey: John Henry Newman 1801-1845* (New York: Paulist, 2001); Sheridan Gilley, *Newman and His Age* (London: Darton, Longman and Todd, 1990); Ian Ker, *John Henry Newman: A Biography* (New York: Oxford University Press, 1988); Charles Stephen Dessain, *John Henry Newman* (London: Nelson, 1966); Meriol Trevor, *Newman: The Pillar of the Cloud* (London: Macmillan, 1962) and *Newman: Light in Winter* (Garden City, NY: Doubleday, 1963); and Maisie Ward, *Young Mr. Newman* (New York: Sheed and Ward, 1948). The classic biography of the Roman Catholic Newman is Wilfrid Ward, *The Life of John Henry Cardinal Newman*, 2 vols. (London: Longmans, Green, 1912).

CHAPTER I

1. *Apo.*, 1. On Newman's 1816 conversion, see Stephen Dessain, "Newman's First Conversion," in *Newman Studien*, ed. H. Fries and W. Becker (Nürnberg: Glock und Lutz, 1957), 3:37-53; and Terrence Merrigan, "*Numquam minus solus, quám cúm solus*—Newman's First Conversion," *Downside Review* 103 (1985): 99-116. (Merrigan's version of the Latin quotation varies slightly from Newman's in *Apo.*, 14, which varies from Cicero's in *De officiis*, III. 1.)

2. *LD* 20:46 (to Mrs. John Mozley, 24 Sept 1861) and 3:172 (to Mrs. Newman, 29 Dec 1832).

3. *LD* 1:3 (from Mr. Newman to JHN, 24 Nov 1806).

4. On Newman's introversion, see Merrigan, "*Numquam minus solus*," 102-06.

5. *LD* 1:16 (to Jemima Newman, 12 Apr 1815).

6. Anne Mozley, "John Henry Newman: His Childhood and School Life," in *Letters and Correspondence of John Henry Newman during his Life in the English Church*, 2 vols., ed. A. Mozley (London: Longmans, Green, 1891), 1: 1-25, at 16, quoting an anecdote from a conversation with "Dr. Newman's [unnamed] sister in her last illness" (Trevor, *Pillar*, 9, identifies the sister as Jemima).

7. James W. Fowler, "Stages in Faith: The Structural-Developmental Approach," in Thomas C. Hennessy, ed., *Values and Moral Development* (New York: Paulist, 1976), 173-211, at 175, 184.

8. *AW*, 169.

9. Kegan, 95. Owen Chadwick comments that Newman "was a solitary by intelligence; a friend but not sociable; one who had compassion for the

people and yet was no man for the multitude" (*Newman* [Oxford: Oxford University Press, 1983], 9).

10. From Mrs. Newman to E. Newman, quoted in M. Ward, 18-19.

11. *AW,* 268, 150.

12. Ibid., 250.

13. Quoted in Trevor, *Pillar,* 17, from an 1859 meditation.

14. *LD* 10:260 (to J. Keble, 8 June 1844) and 31:31 (to A. Mozley, 19 Feb 1885).

15. *Apo.* quotations in the next four paragraphs are from pp. 3-7. Gilley, 24, writes: "The Calvinist experience of conversion was the beginning of Newman's mature devotional life; the dogmas of Calvinism were the beginning of his intellectual life. Doctrine was the objective correlative to a living experience; but Christianity was about the life of the mind as well as about the life of the heart." Dessain, *John Henry Newman,* 5, comments that to Newman "The visible world, so beautiful and significant, seemed less real than that which was unseen. This was not," in Dessain's estimation, "a kind of incipient idealism, but a deep *Christian* way of thinking." Newman's "objective Trinitarian faith kept him from subjective contemplation of himself, and indeed he was a man of action."

16. In his perceptive analysis of Newman's first conversion, Louis Bouyer, himself a convert to the Catholic Church and an Oratorian, sees in Newman's "myself and my Creator" the "crux, the mysterious element of this conversion" (*Newman: His Life and Spirituality,* trans. J. L. May [New York: Meridian Books, 1960], 23). Bouyer emphasizes the young Newman's "strong sense of self, of independence, of self-reliance" as natural, not religious, Christian. "What [Newman] found was that, when this independent spirit, this innate self-reliance of his, was brought into the presence of Another, of God, it meant nothing more nor less than the negation of meaning. How, then, did it come about that this 'self,' so adamant in its nature, was suddenly projected into the 'self' of that Other and became wholly obedient to Him?" (ibid.). Bouyer's answer is that Newman was grasped by "the revelation that God was there, within him, in those very gifts ... which were his strength and support," that "moral consciousness is the consciousness, the awareness, of Someone, of God" (24). The young Newman's understanding of the union of truth and goodness in God was "now one with his affirmation of self" (ibid.). Bouyer's insight here makes no explicit reference to any developmental differentiation of self.

17. *AW,* 150.

18. Blehl, *Pilgrim Journey,* Appendix of Prayers (17 Nov 1817), 410. For a fine selection of Newman's spiritual writings and an excellent brief introduction to his life and spirituality, see Lawrence S. Cunningham, ed., *John*

Henry Newman: Heart Speaks to Heart (Hyde Park, NY: New City Press, 2004).

19. This and following quotations in this paragraph are from *AW*, 79, 80, 165. On the range and variety of Evangelical understandings of conversion in this period, see Gilley, 21-22. Gilley sees "Newman's discovery of God" as "a rediscovery of the deepest neo-Platonic yearnings of his childhood" (20). Newman's first conversion, he states, "was not, in Protestant terms, a wholly new beginning, but a reassertion of the sensations of an earlier one. Calvinist Evangelicalism gave these sensations an intellectual sanction; but the experience which it validated was not an Evangelical conversion at all" (21).

20. Lonergan, 237-38, 131. Dessain, *John Henry Newman*, 5, writes that Newman "was 'made a Christian,' he began a new life. He accepted Revealed Religion in the purest form available to him, and gave himself to God in consequence. It was this turning-point which was to give the rest of his life its unity. His unfolding mind was captured by the Christian Revelation, and his heart by the Christian ideal of holiness."

21. Lonergan, 240.

22. Ibid.

CHAPTER 2

1. See my *Christian Conversion*, 116-28. On Newman's various conversions, see Avery Dulles, "Newman: The Anatomy of a Conversion," in Ian Ker, ed., *Newman and Conversion* (Notre Dame, IN: University of Notre Dame Press, 1997), 21-36.

2. See Gilley, 31. Also see Martin X. Moleski, *Personal Catholicism: The Theological Epistemologies of John Henry Newman and Michael Polanyi* (Washington, DC: Catholic University of America Press, 2000).

3. M. Ward, 48.

4. See Ker, 13-14, and Gilley, 36, about a possible "under the line" third class honors in classics.

5. *LD* 1:118 (to Harriett Newman, 19 Jan 1822). See Gilley, 35, on tension in Newman between intellectual and moral-spiritual excellence.

6. *LD* 1:100 (to Mrs. Newman, 28 Mar 1821).

7. *AW*, 80, 166-67.

8. See esp. Blehl, 35, on prayer, and M. Ward, 59, on sexual temptations.

9. *AW*, 179, 82. See original journal entry (6 Jan 1822) in ibid., 179.

10. Ibid., 180.

11. Ibid., 183.

12. Exchange between JHN and his mother in *LD* 1:122-24, at 124 (from Mrs. Newman to JHN, 11 Mar 1822) and (to Mrs. Newman, 12 Mar 1822).

13. *AW*, 63.

14. Ibid., 65-66.

15. *Apo.*, 10.

16. *AW*, 68.

17. *Apo.*, 10.

18. *AW*, 68.

19. *Apo.*, 14, from *De officiis*, III. 1: "Never less alone [lonely], than when alone [solitary]."

20. *AW*, 71.

21. Ibid., 71, 172; see *John Henry Newman Sermons 1824-1843*, vol. 2, ed. V. F. Blehl (Oxford: Clarendon, 1993), 309-15 (Newman preached "Sins against Conscience" twelve times in seven churches between 1825 and 1843).

22. *AW*, 73.

23. Ibid.

24. *Apo.*, 7.

25. *AW*, 77.

26. *Apo.*, 8.

27. *AW*, 202, 203, 204, 78.

28. Ibid., 79, 206, 78.

29. Ibid., 202, 203.

30. *Apo.*, 11-12. Also see *AW*, 69.

31. *Apo.*, 9.

32. *AW*, 78. Also see Gilley, 57 and Trevor, *Pillar*, 59.

33. *Apo.*, 9, 8.

34. *AW*, 78.

35. *Apo.*, 8-9.

36. *AW*, 206.

37. Trevor, *Pillar*, 59.

38. *AW*, 82. Newman deleted two paragraphs containing these quotations in the autograph.

39. Ibid., 83.

40. *Apo.*, 12.

41. *LD* 1:254 (to C. R. Newman, 25 Aug 1825).

42. Ibid., 1:219 (to C. R. Newman, 24 Mar 1825).

43. *Apo.*, 13.

44. Ibid., 14.

45. *AW*, 212.

46. Ibid., 213.

47. *LD* 2:69 (to Jemima Newman, 10 May 1828).

48. For an assessment of the Oriel influence, especially on Newman's understanding of the relationship between faith and reason, see Terrence Merrigan, "Newman's Oriel Experience: Its Significance for His Life and Thought," *Bijdragen, tijdschrift voor filosofie en theologie* 47 (1986): 192-211.

49. *AW*, 203, 208.

50. *LD* 1:282 (to Mrs. Newman, 31 Mar 1826).

51. See M. Ward, 147.

52. See Gilley, 59.

53. *Apo.*, 21, 22.

54. Ibid., 23.

55. *LD* 2:60 (to J. B. White, 1 Mar 1828).

56. *Apo.*, 16.

57. Ibid.

58. *AW*, 91.

59. *Apo.*, 16, 17, 18.

60. Ibid., 6, 12, 23, 24, 25-26.

61. *AW*, 92; also see 90, 93.

62. Ker, 49. For an introduction to Newman's relationship to the early Christian writers, see Brian E. Daley, "The Church Fathers," in *The Cambridge Companion to John Henry Newman*, ed. I. Ker and T. Merrigan (New York: Cambridge University Press, 2009), 29-46. For a helpful perspective on the *Arians*, see Rowan Williams, "Newman's *Arians* and the Question of Method in Doctrinal History," in Ian Ker and Alan G. Hill, eds., *Newman after a Hundred Years* (Oxford: Clarendon, 1990), 263-85. While acknowledging the limitations of *Arians*, Williams, 263, writes that "Newman ... is making the kind of *methodological* advance that will, on the one hand, make the writing of doctrinal history a more serious and scientific discipline, and on the other, render theologically suspect any attempt to treat as normative the theological ethos and idiom of an earlier age."

63. *AW*, 268.

64. Ibid., 121-22.

65. Ibid., 136. Robert C. Christie, "The Logic of Conversion: The Harmony of Heart, Will, Mind, and Imagination in John Henry Newman" (Ph.D. diss., Fordham University, 1998), 306, interprets Newman's experience in Sicily as an affective conversion, leading to a "moral conversion in his assertion of the image of a reformed Church of England … ." My interpretation sees it as a vocational intensification.

66. *Apo.*, 32.

67. Ibid., 1-2, 4.

68. See Terrence Merrigan, *Clear Heads and Holy Hearts: The Religious and Theological Ideal of John Henry Newman*, Louvain Theological & Pastoral Monographs, 7 (Louvain: Peeters, 1991), 23-29. Also see Louis Dupré, "Newman and the Neoplatonic Tradition in England," in Terrence Merrigan and Ian T. Ker, eds., *Newman and the Word* (Louvain: Peeters, 2000), 137-54.

69. For Thomas Merton's use of this true north image in his autobiography, see my *Christian Conversion*, 174-76.

70. *AW*, 183.

71. About the Peel and tutorial events as they related to Hawkins, David Newsome, *The Convert Cardinals: John Henry Newman and Henry Edward Manning* (London: John Murray, 1993), 62, writes: "As [Newman] emerged from his shell, however, the reserve and deference of earlier years turned only too swiftly to a somewhat unbecoming belligerence." Edward E. Kelly, "Identity and Discourse: A Study in Newman's Individualism," in Gerard Magill, ed., *Discourse and Context: An Interdisciplinary Study of John Henry Newman* (Carbondale: Southern Illinois University Press, 1993), 15-32, at 17, speaks of Newman's "self-protective personality." David Nicholls, "Individualism and the Appeal to Authority," in *Reason, Rhetoric and Romanticism*, 194-213, argues for a moral individualism, a radical Cartesianism in Newman, 194, 196. About "myself and my Creator," he writes: "This psychic individualism, this feeling, to which he referred, is related to the much wider—metaphysical, epistemological and social—individualism which characterizes his writings," 195.

72. See my *Christian Conversion*, 57.

73. See David Goslee, *Romanticism and the Anglican Newman* (Athens: Ohio University Press, 1996), chap. 1, "Parents, Mentors, Siblings, and Friends," 18-41, and on Newman's celibacy, 124-27. On family relationships, also see Newsome, 26-27, and M. Ward, 1-22, 117-31, 161-75.

CHAPTER 3

1. *Apo.*, 32. In a letter to his mother about the upcoming Mediterranean trip, Newman had written: "I really do *not* wish (I think) that this present cessation [from labour] should be any thing else than a preparation and strengthening-time for future toil—rather, I should rejoice to think that I was in this way steeling myself in soul and body for it" (*LD* 3:123 [to Mrs. Newman, 3 Dec 1832]).

2. See Ker, 81. Newman did not attend the 25-29 July 1833 meeting at H. J. Rose's rectory in Hadleigh, Suffolk; Oxford was represented by Hurrell Froude and William Palmer of Worcester College (see Gilley, 113). Newman's interest in parliamentary interference in church and university affairs may be an exception to his general political attitude; see Edward Norman, "Newman's Social and Political Thinking," in *Newman after a Hundred Years*, 153-73, who portrays Newman as "largely unconcerned with the political" (156), and with "a reluctance to espouse social and political causes" (157) and a dislike of "the democratic principle" (168).

3. Ker, 92.

4. *Apo.*, 44, 261, 45.

5. Ibid., 45.

6. Ibid., 47-48, 50.

7. Ibid., 52.

8. Ibid., 53.

9. *LD* 5:83 (R. D. Hampden to JHN, 23 June 1835).

10. Ibid., 5:251 (to S. L. Pope, 3 Mar 1836).

11. *Apo.*, 54.

12. *LD* 5:240-41 (to Jemima Newman, 21 Feb 1836), 263 (to Miss M. R. Giberne, 20 Mar 1836), 249 (to J. W. Bowden, 2 Mar 1836), 253 (to J. Keble, 6 Mar 1836).

13. Ibid., 5:154 (to R. H. Froude, 18 Oct 1835), 64 (to H. Wilberforce, 3 May 1835).

14. Ibid., 4:301 (to T. Mozley, 11 July 1834); 5:110, n. 1 (from Newman's "Extract from account of my illness in Sicily. Littlemore, March 25, 1840").

15. See M. Ward, 248.

16. *Apo.*, 63. During the course of the Oxford Movement, Newman, relying on the Anglican theology of the seventeenth-century Caroline Divines, proposed various versions of Anglo-Catholicism as a *Via Media*: (1) between Liberalism and Evangelicalism within the Church of England (*Apo.*, 93); (2) between Protestantism and Roman Catholicism amidst

the churches (*Apo.*, 62-63); and (3) between Roman Catholicism and Rationalistic unbelief beyond the churches (*Ess.*, 307). From this threefold schema the second version became Newman's principal meaning of *Via Media*. See Anglican parties etc. in next section below.

17. John Henry Cardinal Newman, *The Via Media of the Anglican Church*, 2 vols. (London: Longmans, Green, 1901, 1908), 1:51, 56; hereafter *VM* (also see annotated edition of vol. 1, ed. H. D. Weidner [Oxford: Clarendon, 1990], 99, 103). The 1837 *Lectures on the Prophetical Office of the Church* became the first volume of *The Via Media* in 1877, with Newman's new Preface.

18. See *VM*, 1:268-70. Also see Avery Dulles, "The Threefold Office in Newman's Ecclesiology," in *Newman after a Hundred Years*, 375-99, at 377.

19. John Henry Cardinal Newman, *Lectures on the Doctrine of Justification* (London: Longmans, Green, 1924), 138; hereafter *Jfc*. For a survey of Newman's developing thought on justification, see Thomas L. Sheridan, "Justification," in *Cambridge Companion to JHN*, 98-117. Also see Henry Chadwick, "The *Lectures on Justification*," in *Newman after a Hundred Years*, 287-308.

20. *Jfc.*, 21, 26, 325.

21. *LD* 5:241 (to Jemima Newman, 21 Feb 1836).

22. *Apo.*, 86.

23. John Henry Cardinal Newman, *Essays Critical and Historical*, 2 vols. (Longmans, Green, 1919 [1871]), 1:263-307, at 295, 306; hereafter *Ess.* The 1839 article is here re-titled "Prospects of the Anglican Church."

24. *Apo.*, 94.

25. *Ess.*, 1:307.

26. *Apo.*, 97.

27. Ibid., 95, 104. Monophysitism, as strictly formulated by Eutyches, insisted on a single nature in Christ, with divinity absorbing humanity. This position was rejected as heretical by the Council of Chalcedon (451), whose definition of two natures in the one person of Christ was confirmed by Pope Leo. Imperial and ecclesiastical politics then left the moderately Monophysite Eastern communion in schism. Newman's point of historical analogy was about the alignment of the three parties in the controversy, not about their differences in doctrine.

28. Ibid., 106-07.

29. Ibid., 108, 107.

30. Ibid., 108, 109, 110, 111.

31. See *British Critic* article in *Ess.*, 2:1-73; see *LD* 7:245 (to Mrs. J. Mozley, 25 Feb 1840).

32. *LD* 7:368 (to W. C. A. Maclaurin, 26 July 1840); also see 7:354-55, 363-64 (to R. Williams, 11, 19 July 1840).

33. Ibid., 7:451 (to F. Rogers, 25 Nov 1840).

34. *Ess.*, 2:192.

35. John Henry Cardinal Newman, *Discussions and Arguments on Various Subjects*, ed. J. Tolhurst and G. Tracey (Notre Dame, IN: University of Notre Dame Press, 2004 [1872]), 304.

36. *LD* 8:68 (to A. P. Perceval, 12 Mar 1841).

37. *Apo.*, 118. Peter Nockles, "Oxford, Tract 90 and the Bishops," in *Reason, Rhetoric and Romanticism*, 28-87, offers a revisionist interpretation of the *Tract 90* controversy as he distinguishes Newman's personal odyssey from the wider Oxford Movement.

38. *VM*, 2:271-72, 344.

39. Ibid., 2:397.

40. *Ess.*, 2:338, 337, 338.

41. *Apo.*, 126.

42. Ibid., 129, 132.

43. Ibid., 135, 136-38, 138.

44. Ibid., 142; *LD* 8:375 (to S. F. Wood, 13 Dec 1841). I quote from *LD*, which varies slightly from *Apo.*

45. *Apo.*, 142.

46. Ibid., 155, 147.

47. See Ker, 254, 270.

48. *LD* 9:328 (to J. Keble, 4 May 1843).

49. *Apo.*, 200; *LD* 9:585 (to H. E. Manning, 25 Oct 1843). I quote from *LD*, which varies slightly from *Apo.* For "The Parting of Friends" (25 Sept 1843), see John Henry Newman, *Sermons bearing on Subjects of the Day* (London: Longmans, Green, 1918 [1843]), 395-409.

50. *Apo.*, 207. For letters in this paragraph, see *LD* 10:129-30 (to J. W. Bowden, 21 Feb 1844), 126 (to E. B. Pusey, 19 Feb 1844), 101-03 (to J. Keble, 23 Jan 1844), 53, 189-92, 195-98, 200-04, 237-44, 251 (to Mrs. W. Froude, 9 Dec 1843; 4, 5, 9 Apr 1844; 19, 28 May 1844), 263, 298-99 (to H. Wilberforce, 8 June 1844; 17 July 1844), 390 (to Miss M. R. Giberne, 7 Nov 1844), 412-13 (to H. E. Manning, 16 Nov 1844).

51. *LD* 10:595-98 (to Mrs. J. Mozley, 15 Mar 1845).

52. Ibid., 10:723 (to E. Coleridge, 3 July 1845), 729 (to R. Westmacott, 11 July 1845).

53. *Dev.*, 159. See Nicholas Lash, *Newman on Development: The Search for an Explanation in History* (Shepherdstown, WV: Patmos, 1975). For a brief introduction to Newman on development, see Gerard H. McCarren, "Development of doctrine," in *Cambridge Companion to JHN, 118-36.* For a contemporary application of the tests, see Gerald O'Collins, "Newman's Seven Notes: The Case of the Resurrection," in *Newman after a Hundred Years,* 337-52. For a critical view of the *Essay* as unpersuasive and of the set of tests as something "no one ever believed in," see Owen Chadwick, *Newman*, 45-48.

54. *Apo.*, 212. J.-H. Walgrave interrelates personal and historical development throughout his *Newman the Theologian*, trans. A. V. Littledale (New York: Sheed & Ward, 1960 [1957]).

55. *Dev.*, xl.

56. *LD* 10:771 (to E. Hawkins, 3 Oct 1845).

57. *Apo.*, 216. Jeffrey D. Marlett, "Conversion Methodology and the Case of Cardinal Newman," *Theological Studies* 58/4 (December 1997): 669-85, emphasizes the context of conversion; he focuses on Newman's ecclesial conversion, with brief mention of his adolescent conversion and no direct reference to his cognitive conversion to Anglo-Catholicism.

58. These "moments" or "poles" of deconversion and conversion are often on-going dimensions of a single extended process. For a sociological analysis of deconversion in terms of social role change, see Helen Rose Fuchs Ebaugh, *Becoming an Ex: The Process of Role Exit* (Chicago: University of Chicago Press, 1988), which delineates the process of role disengagement and disidentification (as well as identity reestablishment in a new role as an "ex") in four phases: First Doubts, Seeking Alternatives, The Turning Point, and Creating the Ex-Role. For an excellent analysis of conversion from social scientific perspectives, see Lewis R. Rambo, *Understanding Religious Conversion* (New Haven: Yale University Press, 1993). John D. Barbour, *Versions of Deconversion: Autobiography and the Loss of Faith* (Charlottesville: University Press of Virginia, 1994), 25, discusses Newman's deconversion in terms of what Rambo names "institutional transition" or "denominational switching." For hermeneutical attention to the historical, cultural, and metaphorical dimensions of conversion, see Karl F. Morrison, *Understanding Conversion* (Charlottesville: University Press of Virginia, 1992).

59. Frank M. Turner, *John Henry Newman: The Challenge to Evangelical Religion* (New Haven: Yale University Press, 2002). For a brief introduction to this 740-page tome, see the helpful review by Edward J. Enright (*Newman Studies Journal* 1/1 [Spring 2004]: 77-78). The core of Turner's

argument is also presented in the 115-page Introduction to his new edition of Newman's *Apologia pro Vita Sua and Six Sermons* (New Haven: Yale University Press, 2008).

60. See, e.g., *Apo.*, 27, 28, 30, 37, 44, 52, 53, 95, 173, 184. For a recent overview directed to our contemporary theological context, see Terrence Merrigan, "Newman and Theological Liberalism," *Theological Studies* 66/3 (September 2005): 605-21. For Newman on Evangelicalism, see, e.g., *Apo.*, 28, 58, 80, 85, esp. 93-94.

61. *Apo.*, 259-69, at 259.

62. Turner, 23, 7.

63. *Ess.*, 1:33, 95 ("On the Introduction of Rationalistic Principles into Revealed Religion," 30-101, originally written in 1835 and published in 1836 as Number 73 of *Tracts for the Times*). See also Newman's critique of the Evangelical introverted focus on "a certain state of heart" rather than looking "unto Jesus" in Sermon 15, "Self-Contemplation," in his *Parochial and Plain Sermons*, 2:163-74, at 166, 163.

64. *Ess.*, 1:34.

65. *Apo.*, 123 (first brackets in text; second brackets my addition); see *LD* 7:433-34 (to J. Keble, 6 Nov 1840). *Apo.* text has "spirit" in brackets after "Protestant"; in *LD*, the Greek ἦθος follows "Protestant."

66. *Apo.*, 173; see *LD* 8:269-70 (to A. L. Phillipps, 12 Sept 1841).

67. John Henry Newman, *Fifteen Sermons Preached before the University of Oxford between A.D. 1826 and 1843*, intro. Mary Katherine Tillman (Notre Dame, IN: University of Notre Dame Press, 1997 [1843; 3rd ed., 1872]), 54-74, at 55, 58; hereafter *US* (also see annotated edition, *Newman: Oxford University Sermons* on spine, ed. J. D. Earnest and G. Tracey [New York: Oxford University Press, 2006], 49, 50-51). See Merrigan, "Newman's Oriel Experience," 206-09.

68. *US*, 187, 188, 189, 191, 199-200. For an introductory survey of Newman on faith, see Thomas J. Norris, "Faith," in *Cambridge Companion to JHN*, 73-97. For a very helpful analysis of Newman on faith, reason, and certitude, see John R. Connolly, *John Henry Newman: A View of Catholic Faith for the New Millennium* (Lanham, MD: Rowman & Littlefield, 2005).

69. *US*, 203, 207, 206, 213, 215, 250, 236, 239.

70. Ibid., 257, 259; see 193.

71. See *Apo.*, 108, 171. On the complexity and ambiguity of the relationship between faith and imagination, see M. Jamie Ferreira, "The Grammar of the Heart: Newman on Faith and Imagination," in *Discourse and Context*, 129-43.

72. *Apo.*, 102.

146 Conscience & Conversion in Newman

73. Ibid., 104, 107, 108. The independence of mind suggested by "for myself" also points to Fowler's faithing Stage 4.

74. Ibid., 111, 110, 114.

75. Ibid., 133, 134.

76. Ibid., 152, 153.

77. Ibid., 167, 194.

78. Ibid., 180, 181.

79. Ibid., 181.

80. Ibid., 194, 195, 206, 207.

81. Ibid., 207, 208; see LD 10:412-13 (to H. E. Manning, 16 Nov 1844). I quote from LD, which varies slightly from Apo., where Manning is not identified.

82. Apo., 208, 209, 210, 212; see LD 10:390, 484-85, 610 (to Miss M. R. Giberne, 7 Nov 1844, 8 Jan 1845, 30 Mar 1845). I quote from LD, which varies slightly from Apo.

83. Apo., 216, 217.

84. Ibid., 104; see 121, 134, 147, 160-61, 193, 197.

85. Turner, 6, 11, 21.

86. Ibid., 529, 542, 548.

87. Ibid., 622-23.

88. Apo., 171, 181, 206, 207, 195.

89. Ibid., 104, 106, 107, 108, 109; see 44-51.

90. Ibid., 124, 132, 142.

91. Ibid., 141.

92. Ibid., 141, 142.

93. Quoted in Sue Halpern, "The Gene Hunters," The New Yorker, 12 Dec 2005, pp. 92-93.

94. Apo., 152.

95. For an interpretation of the self as self-transcending, driven ultimately by and to God, see below, chap. 4 and Appendix, and my The Desiring Self (New York: Paulist, 1998). Here I distinguish reflection leading to judgment, discernment leading to judgment of conscience, and deliberation leading to decision.

96. Apo., 200.

97. Ibid., 209.

CHAPTER 4

1. See *AW*, 239-42, 245-48, for Newman's pre-ordination retreat notes (8-17 Apr 1847), where he describes a "wound or cancer" in his mind.

2. *LD* 12:381-82 (to H. Wilberforce, 25 [9] Dec 1848).

3. See Ker, 347, 349, 360.

4. John Henry Cardinal Newman, *Certain Difficulties felt by Anglicans in Catholic Teaching*, 2 vols. (London: Longmans, Green, 1920), 1:186, 368-71; hereafter *Diff*.

5. See Ker, 399. Trial costs, amounting to some £10,000, were more than covered by donations from generous Catholics around the world, acknowledged by Newman in his dedication of the first part of *The Idea of a University*; see *AW*, 13, 268 and W. Ward, *Life*, 1:303.

6. *LD* 14:257, n. 2 (Archbishop Cullen to JHN, 15 Apr 1851). For Newman's experience in Dublin, see his "Memorandum about My Connection with the Catholic University," in *AW*, 277-333; and Colin Barr, *Paul Cullen, John Henry Newman, and the Catholic University of Ireland, 1845-1865* (Notre Dame, IN: University of Notre Dame Press, 2003).

7. See *LD* 14:389-90 (to Mrs. W. Froude, 14 Oct 1851), where Newman views the Dublin university as a new phase in the fight against Liberalism.

8. Ibid., 16:535 (to Mrs. J. W. Bowden, 31 Aug 1855).

9. Ibid., 15:28 (to Archbishop Cullen, 4 Feb 1852). See John Henry Cardinal Newman, *The Idea of a University* (London: Longmans, Green, 1909 [1852, 1858, 3rd ed. 1873]); hereafter *Idea*.

10. See Ker, 410.

11. *LD* 17:71 (to A. St. John, 18 Nov 1855); 17:139 (diary entry, 29 Jan 1856).

12. See Ker, 420-22.

13. John Henry Newman, *On Consulting the Faithful in Matters of Doctrine*, ed. J. Coulson (London: Geoffrey Chapman, 1961 [1859, 1871]), 63. Also see Ker, 486.

14. See *LD* 20:328 (to A. St. John, 25 Oct 1862); 19:280-83 (Newman's Memorandum, The Delation to Rome, 14 Jan 1860).

15. *AW*, 254; *LD* 20:215-16 (to the Editor of the *Globe*, 28 June 1862).

16. See *LD* 20:398 (to C. A. Bathurst, 21 Jan 1863).

17. Ibid., 20:571 (quoted in Newman's letter to Messrs. Macmillan and Co., 30 Dec 1863).

18. *Apo.*, 216, 217. Newman did believe in the Real Presence as an Anglican.

19. *LD* 23:187 (to J. Wallis, 23 Apr 1867); see 23:189 (to J. L. Patterson, 25 Apr 1867). On theological liberty of Roman Catholics, see Edward J. Miller, *John Henry Newman on the Idea of Church* (Shepherdstown, WV: Patmos, 1987), 81-98. On Manning, see Newsome, *Convert Cardinals*, and Edward Jeremy Miller, "Newman and Manning: The Strained Relationship," *Horizons* 35/2 (Fall 2008): 228-52.

20. *AW*, 270.

21. *LD* 24:91-92 (to P. Renouf, 21 June 1868). See Francis A. Sullivan, "Newman on Infallibility," in *Newman after a Hundred Years*, 419-46, and id., "Infallibility," in *Cambridge Companion to JHN*, 156-69.

22. *LD* 24:325 (to Mrs. Helbert, 30 Aug 1869).

23. Ibid., 24:354-55 (to Mrs. Helbert, 20 Oct 1869).

24. Ibid., 25:18-19 (to Bishop Ullathorne, 28 Jan 1870), 64 (to W. Monsell, 23 Mar 1870).

25. Ibid., 25:175 (to W. J. O'Neill Daunt, 7 Aug 1870); see 25:192 (to A. St. John, 21 Aug 1870), 299 (to Mrs. W. Froude, 5 Mar 1871), 245 (to W. Monsell, 12 Dec 1870).

26. Ibid., 25:277 (to Miss Holmes, 29 Jan 1871); 27:122, n. 3 (Gladstone quoted in editor's note). For the *Letter's* context, see John T. Ford, "Newman's *Letter to the Duke of Norfolk*: Citizenship, Church, and Conscience," *Josephinum Journal of Theology* 8/2 (Summer/Fall 2001): 38-50. It was also in 1875 that the Jesuit Gerard Manley Hopkins, who as an Oxford student had been received into the Roman Catholic Church by Newman in 1866, wrote in revolutionary sprung rhythm his poem *The Wreck of the Deutschland* in memory of five German Franciscan nuns bound for America who died with many others in a North Sea shipwreck. Hopkins had taught at the Birmingham Oratory School for one year before joining the Jesuits.

27. John Henry Cardinal Newman, *A Letter addressed to the Duke of Norfolk, on occasion of Mr. Gladstone's Expostulation of 1874*, in *Diff.*, 2:179, 341-42, 342; see 2:176-77, 332-39.

28. Ibid., 2:243, 244.

29. Ibid., 2:245, 246.

30. Ibid., 2:246, 247.

31. Ibid., 2:247, 250; see 252, 253.

32. Ibid., 2:255, 256, 257; see 258. John Finnis, "Conscience in the *Letter to the Duke of Norfolk*," in *Newman after a Hundred Years*, 401-18, citing negative universal moral norms, argues that Newman is wrong in concluding that "conscience cannot come into direct collision with the Church's or the Pope's infallibility" (414-15). For a rejoinder that "Finnis systematically

misinterprets Newman" and misunderstands his theory of moral judgment, see Gerard J. Hughes, "Newman and the Particularity of Conscience," in Ian Ker and Terrence Merrigan, eds., *Newman and Faith* (Louvain: Peeters, 2004), 53-74.

33. See *Diff.*, 2:256-57, 261; 259, 261. For a critical view of Newman on the relation between papal authority and personal conscience, see Fergus Kerr, "Did Newman Answer Gladstone?" in *Reason, Rhetoric and Romanticism*, 135-52.

34. Other authors who present different threefold interpretations of conscience include: Louis Monden, *Sin, Liberty and Law*, trans. J. Donceel (New York: Sheed and Ward, 1965), 5, 7, 9, also 102-11; John Macquarrie, *Three Issues in Ethics* (New York: Harper & Row, 1970), 111-17; Timothy E. O'Connell, *Principles for a Catholic Morality*, rev. ed. (San Francisco: HarperSanFrancisco, 1990), 109-14; Richard M. Gula, *Reason Informed by Faith* (New York: Paulist, 1989), 131-33; Russell B. Connors, Jr. and Patrick T. McCormick, *Character, Choices & Community* (New York: Paulist, 1998), 122-30. For brief, comprehensive historical and theoretical treatments of conscience, see Charles E. Curran, *Directions in Fundamental Moral Theology* (Notre Dame, IN: University of Notre Dame Press, 1985), 215-25, and *The Catholic Moral Tradition Today* (Washington, DC: Georgetown University Press, 1999), 172-96.

For recent treatments of conscience in Newman of varying value, see S. A. Grave, *Conscience in Newman's Thought* (Oxford: Clarendon, 1989), Ronald Ledek, *The Nature of Conscience and Its Religious Significance with Special Reference to John Henry Newman* (San Francisco: International Scholars Press, 1996), Nicholas Madden, "Newman: Conscience, The Matrix of Spirituality," *Irish Theological Quarterly* 67 (2002): 145-51, Philip C. Rule, *Coleridge and Newman: The Centrality of Conscience* (New York: Fordham University Press, 2004). For a helpful survey of Newman on conscience, see Gerard J. Hughes, "Conscience," in *Cambridge Companion to JHN*, 189-220. Especially valuable is Edward J. Miller, "Newman on Conscience and Lonergan on Conversion: The Shadow of Plato," in *Critical Essays on John Henry Newman*, ed. E. Block, Jr., English Literary Studies, 55 (Victoria, BC: University of Victoria, 1992), 105-19, esp. 112-18 on "self-correcting conscience."

35. *LD* 1:170 (to C. R. Newman, 12 Dec 1823); *Sermon Notes of John Henry Cardinal Newman 1849-1878*, ed. Fathers of the Birmingham Oratory (London: Longmans, Green, 1913), 187; hereafter *SN*; John Henry Newman, *Sermons Preached on Various Occasions* (London: Longmans, Green, 1908 [1857]), 65; hereafter *OS*; id., *Parochial and Plain Sermons*, 8 vols. (London: Longmans, Green, 1907 [1868]), 1:227; hereafter *PS*; *SN*, 327; *PS*, 6:339-40. For a detailed consideration of conscience in Newman's *Parochial and Plain Sermons*, see Fabio Attard, "John Henry Newman:

Advocacy of Conscience—1825-1832, and 1833-1843," *Salesianum* 62 (2000): 331-51, 433-56, and 63 (2001): 315-40, 521-36. Also see A. J. Boekraad, *The Personal Conquest of Truth according to J. H. Newman* (Louvain: Editions Nauwelaerts, 1955), esp. 281-303.

36. *PS*, 1:216-17.

37. Ibid., 5:225, 226; 1:250.

38. John Henry Cardinal Newman, *An Essay in Aid of a Grammar of Assent* (London: Longmans, Green, 1903 [1870]), 417; hereafter *GA*; *Apo.*, 198; *OS*, 64; id., *Callista: A Tale of the Third Century* (London: Longmans, Green, 1901[1856]), 314 (new edition with same pagination, intro. A. G. Hill [Notre Dame, IN: University of Notre Dame Press, 2000]).

39. *GA*, 105.

40. Ibid., 105, 106.

41. Ibid., 389-90, 390, 360. Of the Illative Sense, Newman writes: "It is the mind that reasons, and that controls its own reasonings, not any technical apparatus of words and propositions. This power of judging and concluding, when in its perfection, I call the Illative Sense," which, "as exercised by gifted, or by educated or otherwise well-prepared minds, has its function in the beginning, middle, and end of all verbal discussion and inquiry, and in every step of the process. It is a rule to itself, and appeals to no judgment beyond its own ..." (ibid., 353, 361-62).

42. Ibid., 354. On implicit, non-discursive reasoning, see Gerard Magill, "Newman on Liberal Education and Moral Pluralism," *Scottish Journal of Theology* 45 (1992): 45-64, esp. 54-61. Also see Mary Katherine Tillman, "Economies of Reason: Newman and the *Phronesis* Tradition," in *Discourse and Context*, 45-53.

43. *GA*, 354-55, 355. In this passage Newman uses "decide" as equivalent to my "judge," the terminus of the discernment process. In my analysis, "decide" is reserved for the terminus of the subsequent process of deliberation.

44. Ibid., 356. See Joseph Dunne, "J. H. Newman's Appeal to Phronesis in *A Grammar of Assent*," in his *Back to Rough Ground* (Notre Dame, IN: University of Notre Dame Press, 1993), 31-54, esp. 33-38.

45. *LD* 2:280 (to C. R. Newman, 19 Aug 1830). Hugo Meynell, "Newman's Vindication of Faith in the *Grammar of Assent*," in *Newman after a Hundred Years*, 247-61, distinguishes six senses of certitude in Newman, and argues against the negative view of Jay Newman, *The Mental Philosophy of John Henry Newman* (Waterloo, ON: Wilfrid Laurier University Press, 1986).

46. *GA*, 302.

47. *LD* 2:280 (to C. R. Newman, 19 Aug 1830).

48. Ibid., 21:146 (to J. Walker, 6 July 1864).

49. See *GA*, 104.

50. Ibid., 106; *OS*, 64-65.

51. *GA*, 106-07, 107.

52. Ibid., 107-08.

53. Ibid., 108.

54. Ibid., 109, 110, 116-17. See Adrian J. Boekraad and Henry Tristram, *The Argument from Conscience to the Existence of God according to J. H. Newman* (Louvain: Editions Nauwelaerts, 1961); chap. 4 (103-25) is Newman's unpublished 1859 paper "Proof of Theism."

55. See *Idea*, 192.

56. See Lonergan, *Method in Theology*; also see my *Conscience: Development and Self-Transcendence* (Birmingham, AL: Religious Education Press, 1981), *Christian Conversion*, and *The Desiring Self*.

EPILOGUE

1. *LD* 28:290 (to Mother Mary Imelda Poole, 26 Dec 1877). See Erik Sidenvall, *After Anti-Catholicism? John Henry Newman and Protestant Britain, 1845-c.1890* (New York: T&T Clark International, 2005), 99-103.

2. *Apo.*, 215.

3. John Henry Cardinal Newman, "Biglietto Speech," in *Addresses to Cardinal Newman with His Replies, etc. 1879-81*, ed. W. P. Neville (New York: Longmans, Green, 1905), 64.

INDEX

A

Achilli, Giacinto, 98, 102–103

Acton, Sir John, 102–103

Alton, 18, 27

Ambrose, Saint, 21, 42, 52, 78

Analogy, 35–36, 41, 44–47, 142 n.27

Andrewes, Lancelot, 58

Anglo-Catholicism, 8, 26, 56–57, 59, 80, 122, 141 n.16

Antiquity, 42, 57, 60, 88

Apologia pro Vita Sua, 8, 13, 20–22, 32, 36, 38, 40, 42, 46, 52–54, 59–60, 62–67, 69–71, 76–82, 85–87, 90–91, 98, 105–106, 108, 123

Apostolicity, 52, 57, 59, 64, 68, 88

Aquinas, Saint Thomas, 112–113, 121

Arianism, 44, 63, 87, 103

Arians of the Fourth Century, The, 43–44, 52, 139 n.62

Aristotle, 29, 45–46, 113, 116, 121

Athanasius, Saint, 62–63

Augustine, Saint, 21, 42, 60, 62, 75–76, 87, 103, 109, 113, 121

Austen, Jane, 18, 100

Authority, 106–107, 111–112, 118, 131

B

Bagot, Richard, Bishop of Oxford, 58–59, 84

Baptismal regeneration, 34–35, 37, 39–40, 45

Barberi, Dominic, 69

Birmingham, 107. *See also* Oratory of St. Philip Neri; Oratory School, 96–97, 101–102, 104

Bowden, John, 27–28, 55–56, 66, 91

British Critic, 59, 61, 63

British Magazine, 52

Brown, Thomas Joseph, Bishop of Newport, 103

Butler, Joseph, 36, 41, 45–46, 49

C

Callista, 102, 115

Calvin, John (Calvinism), 20, 29, 32, 34–35, 38, 40, 136 n.15, 137 n.19,

Cambridge University, 27, 54

Catholicity (Catholic Church, Catholicism), 35, 37, 44, 57–62, 64, 66, 68–69, 71, 73, 75–76, 79, 83, 89–90, 93–94, 101

"Catholicity of the Anglican Church, The," 61

Catholic University of Ireland, 8, 98, 100–101

Certain Difficulties Felt by Anglicans in Catholic Teaching, 98

Certitude (Certainty), 42, 52–53, 65, 79–80, 82, 85–86, 90, 94, 108, 114, 117–118

Character, 8, 74–75, 125, 132–133

Christian Observer, 30

Church of England (Anglican), 7–8, 13, 20, 26–27, 37, 42, 53, 56–67, 69–70, 73, 75–76, 78–79, 81–87,

89–95, 98, 103–104, 106, 108, 110, 123, 128, 141 n.16

"Church of the Fathers, Letters on the," 52

Church, Richard, 56, 67, 84

Cicero, 29, 32, 138 n.19

Conscience, 8–9, 16, 24–25, 33–34, 47, 53, 62, 81–82, 86, 89–91, 94–95, 102–103, 104, 106, 111–123, 125–126, 132–133, 148 n.32

Conversion, 7, 9, 19–25, 29, 34, 45, 69, 83, 102, 107, 125–129, 133

　Affective Conversion, 23, 25, 128–130, 140

　Basic (Christian) Moral Conversion, 7, 8, 24–26, 47, 122, 128–131, 140

　Cognitive Conversion, 8, 23–24, 26–27, 45, 47, 70–72, 75, 77, 89, 122, 128, 130–131

　Critical Moral Conversion, 7, 23–25, 128, 131

　Ecclesial Conversion, 7–8, 26, 70, 73, 76–77, 79, 82, 84–86, 88, 90–91, 93–96, 105, 108–109

　Moral

　Religious Conversion, 7, 24–25, 128, 131–132

Copleston, Edward, 32

Crabbe, George, 28

Cullen, Paul, Archbishop of Armagh (later of Dublin), 98–100

D

Dalgairns, J. D., 69, 85

Daniel, Jack, 7

Darnell, Nicholas, 104

Darwin, Charles, 92

Decision, 86, 90–91, 94–95, 113, 120, 122, 129, 132–133, 146, 150

Deconversion, 8, 69–70, 91, 93, 144

Deliberation, 90, 92, 94–95, 122, 126, 146, 150 n.43

Demand, 113, 118–119, 121–122

Desire, 9, 102, 113–115, 121–122, 125–126

Development, 7–9, 15, 17–18, 22–23, 42, 47–48, 70, 83, 92, 95–96, 102, 125, 127–128, 136

　Affective Development, 15. See also Erikson, Erik

　Cognitive Development, 16, 130. See also Piaget, Jean

　Doctrinal Development, 65–66, 68, 80, 86, 89, 91, 109

　Faith Development, 16, 131. See also Fowler, James

　Moral Development, 16, 23, 130. See also Kohlberg, Lawrence

　Self Development, 17. See also Kegan, Robert

Development of Christian Doctrine, An Essay on the, 67–69, 80, 91, 95

Discernment, 89–90, 94–95, 113, 116, 118, 121–122, 146 n.95, 150 n.43

Dogma, 52–53, 56, 61, 71–72, 87, 108, 110–111

Döllinger, Johann Joseph Ignaz von, 102–103

Donatists, 60

Dublin, 98–101

Dupanloup, Félix, Bishop, 108

E

Ealing School, 14–15, 30

Economy, Principle of, 44

Edgbaston, 97

Egocentrism, 72–73

Elucidations of Dr. Hampden's Theological Statements, 54

Empiricism (Empirical), 23, 35, 45–46, 49, 130

Encyclical Letter, 1864 (*Quanta Cura*), 110

Encyclopedia Metropolitana, 33, 38, 42

Erikson, Erik, 15, 23–24, 47–48, 127–130, 132

    Autonomy, 15

    Generativity, 23, 48, 128, 130

    Identity, 23, 25, 47–48, 50, 127

    Industry, 16

    Initiative, 15–16

    Integrity, 23, 128, 132

    Intimacy, 23, 48, 128, 130

    Trust, 15

Eutyches (Eutychians), 60, 142 n.27

Evangelicalism, 8, 20, 22, 27–30, 33–35, 37–41, 45–46, 49, 52, 57, 59, 68, 70–73, 83, 122, 137 n.19, 141 n.16

F

Faber, F. W., 97, 101, 104

Faith and reason, 73–75, 96, 108

Faussett, D.D., A Letter to the Rev. Godfrey, 58

Faussett, Godfrey, 58

Final perseverance, 20, 46

Fowler, James, 16–17, 24, 49, 128, 131

    Conjunctive (Paradoxical-Consolidative) Faith (Stage 5), 49–50

    Individuative-Reflexive Faith (Stage 4), 24, 49–50, 131

    Intuitive-Projective Faith (Stage 1), 17

    Mythic-Literal Faith (Stage 2), 17

    Synthetic-Conventional Faith (Stage 3), 24, 49, 131

    Universalizing Faith (Stage 6), 24, 131

Francis de Sales, Saint, 123

Franklin, Sir John, 69

Froude, R. Hurrell, 39–41, 43–46, 48, 53, 55–56, 58, 72, 91, 141 n.2

Froude, Mrs. William, 66

G

Gibbon, Edward, 28

Giberne, Maria, 81

Gilley, Sheridan, 9

Gladstone, William, 110–113

Gorham case, 97-98

Grammar of Assent, An Essay in Aid of a, 42, 108, 113, 115, 119

Grey Court House (Ham), 13

H

Hampden, R. D., 54

Hawkins, Edward, 33–37, 39, 41–43, 45–46, 48–49, 69, 72

Home and Foreign Review, 104

Home Thoughts Abroad, 56

Hooker, Richard, 58

Hopkins, Gerard Manley, 148 n.26

Hume, David, 17, 19, 29, 38

I
Idealism, 45–46, 49, 136 n.15

Idea of a University, The, 99–100, 102

Ignatius, Saint, 42

Ignatius of Loyola, Saint, 96

Illative Sense, 116–117, 150 n.41

Imagination, 16, 23, 29, 39, 46–47, 60–61, 66–67, 75–79, 82, 85–87, 93–95, 98, 115, 118, 121

Infallibility, 103, 106, 108–112, 118, 148 n.32

J
James, William (Oriel College), 36, 45

James, William (Varieties), 24

Justification, 57

Justification, Lectures on, 57

Justin, Saint, 42

K
Keble, John, 19, 32, 39, 41, 43–46, 48–49, 51, 55, 58, 61, 66, 72–73, 85, 91, 109

Kegan, Robert, See also Self, 17, 23, 50, 128, 130

Ker, Ian, 9, 44, 52

Kingsley, Charles, 105–106

Kohlberg, Lawrence, 16, 23, 48–49, 128–132. See also Moral Reasoning

L
Latitudinarianism, 38

Laud, William, 58

"Lead, Kindly Light," 51

Leo XIII, Pope, 123

Leo the Great, Pope Saint, 142 n.27

Liberalism, 31, 38–42, 44–46, 49, 51–54, 59, 61–62, 70–74, 83, 110, 123, 141 n.16

Lincoln's Inn, 28

Littlemore, 56, 61, 63, 65–66, 69, 79, 84–86, 89–90, 93, 96–97

Lloyd, Charles, 33, 39

Locke, John, 28, 45–46

Lockhart, William, 90, 93

Lonergan, Bernard, 23, 125

Loss and Gain, 97

Luther, Martin, 38, 57

Lyra Apostolica, 52

M
Macmillan's Magazine, 105

Manning, Henry, 66, 80, 98, 107–108, 110, 113

Maryvale, 97

Mayers, Walter, 20, 22, 30, 72

Melbourne, Lord, 54

Memoir (JHN's 1874), 30, 33, 35, 37, 44

Merton, Thomas, 7

Middleton, Conyers, 38

Milman, Henry Hart, 62

Milner, Joseph, 21, 42

Monophysites, 60, 63–64, 73, 75–77, 86–87, 142 n.27

Moral reasoning (see also Kohlberg, Lawrence)
    Conventional, 16–17, 49, 128–129

Postconventional, 23, 48–49, 128–129, 131

Preconventional, 128–129

Mozley, John, 56

Mozley, Thomas, 56

Mullens, John, 27

N

Natural moral law, 112, 115

Nelson, Horatio, Viscount 13

Newman, Charles (brother), 13–15, 38, 91

Newman, Elizabeth (aunt), 13, 18

Newman, Elizabeth (grandmother), 13, 18

Newman, Francis (brother), 13, 15, 30, 48, 91

Newman, Harriett (sister, Mrs. Thomas Mozley), 13, 15, 28, 56, 91

Newman, Jemima (sister, Mrs. John Mozley), 13, 15, 39, 56, 67, 91

Newman, John (father), 13–14, 18–19, 27, 30–31, 35, 48, 91

Newman, Mrs. John (mother, Jemima Fourdrinier), 13, 15, 18–19, 31, 35, 56, 91

Newman, Mary (sister), 13, 39, 46, 91

Newton, Thomas, 21

Nicholas, George, 14

Norfolk, Duke of, 110

Norfolk, Letter to the Duke of, 110–111, 113, 118, 123

O

Oakeley, Frederick, 84, 92

On Consulting the Faithful in Matters of Doctrine, 103

Oratory of St. Philip Neri, 97, 99, 101–102, 104, 106–107

Oratory School, 104, 107, 110, 148 n.26

Oriel College, 30–34, 36, 38–41, 43, 48, 54, 56, 69, 72, 78–79, 82, 85–86, 103

Oscott College, 96–97

Oxford Movement. *See* Tractarian Movement

Oxford University (Oxford), 27, 29, 31, 33, 39, 48, 51, 53–56, 65, 70, 91, 96–97, 99, 103, 106–108, 122–124

P

Paine, Thomas, 17, 19

Palmer, William, 141 n.2

Parochial and Plain Sermons, 52

"Parting of Friends, The," 66

Paul, Saint, 21, 34, 114

Peel, Robert, 42–43, 62, 84

Pennsylvania, University of, 124

Phronesis, 113, 116–118

Piaget, Jean, 16, 23, 26, 49, 128–130

    Concrete operations, 16, 130

    Formal operations, 16–17, 129–130

    Preoperational knowing, 16

    Sensorimotor knowing, 16, 130

Pius IX, Pope, 96, 123

Platonism, 13, 29, 46, 137 n.19

Pope, Alexander, 17

Predestination, 20, 29, 40

Present Position of Catholics in England, Lectures on, 98

Private judgment, 56, 61, 63, 72, 111

"Private Judgment," 63

Probability, 36, 41–42, 45, 47, 57, 74–75, 79–80, 90, 108, 117–118

Prophetical Office of the Church, Lectures on the, 56–57

Protestantism, 27, 56–58, 60–61, 63–64, 71, 73, 87, 98, 107, 112, 137 n.19, 141 n.16

Pusey, Edward, 33, 39–40, 45–46, 48, 66, 72, 85, 91

R

Rambler, 102–104

Rationalism, 38, 46, 49, 59, 72–74, 76, 142 n.16

Reason and imagination, 75-78

Record, 52

"Records of the Church," 52

Rednal, 124

Rogers, Frederic, 56, 62

Romaine, William, 20

Roman Catholic Church (Roman Church, Rome), 7–8, 26, 35–36, 40, 44, 53, 56–71, 73, 75–99, 101, 103–110, 112, 122–124, 128, 141 n.16, 142 n.16

Romanticism, 13–14, 28, 59

Rose, Hugh James, 43, 141 n.2

Russell, Charles, 65, 89

S

Sacramental principle, 41–42, 44, 46, 53, 56, 61, 64, 87–88

St. Bartholomew's Eve, 28

St. Benet Fink, Church of, 13

St. Clement's Parish, 33

St. George-Hyslop, Peter, 88

St. John, Ambrose, 96–97, 104, 106, 124

St. Mary the Virgin University Church, 33, 41, 44, 51–52, 56, 61–62, 64, 66, 78–80, 86–87, 89–91

St. Wilfrid's Community (Faber), 97

Scott, Thomas, 21

Scott, Walter, 14, 28, 59

Self, 8, 17–18, 25, 47, 50, 89–92, 95, 115–116, 119, 121–122, 125–127, 129–131, 136 n.16. *See also* Kegan, Robert

    Imperial (2), 17

    Impulsive (1), 17

    Institutional (4), 50

    Interindividual (5), 23, 130

    Interpersonal (3), 17

Self-Transcendence, 27, 122, 125–127, 132–133

Sicily, 44, 51

"Sins against Conscience," 33

Standard, 109

"State of Religious Parties, The," 59

Subjectivism, 71–73

Sumner, John, 34, 45

Superego, 15–16, 121

Syllabus of Errors, 108, 111

Symbol, 16–17, 47, 49–50, 130

T

Thirty-nine Articles, 54, 62, 76, 84

Tractarian Movement, 8, 36, 43–44, 51–53, 55–56, 58, 61–62, 65–67,

70–71, 78, 83–85, 89, 91, 93, 97, 141 n.16

Tract 90, 62–63, 67, 83–84, 87, 92, 103

Tracts for the Times, 51–52, 56, 58–59, 62

Trevor, Meriol, 37, 45

Trinity College, 27, 29–30, 123

Turner, Frank, 70–71, 83–84, 92, 93

U

Ullathorne, W. B., Bishop of Birmingham, 104, 107, 109

Ultramontanism, 106–107, 109–110, 113

Undergraduate, The, 28

University Sermons, 65, 89, 108

"Usurpations of Reason, The," 74

V

Van Pelt, Linus, 26

Vatican Council I, 108–111

Vatican Council II, 8

Via Media, 46–47, 56, 59–65, 73, 86–88, 141 n.16, 142 n.16

Via media

    Between extreme authors, 8

    Epistemological, 46–47

    Norfolk Letter as, 110

    Oratory as, 97

Voltaire, 17, 19

W

Ward, Maisie, 28

Ward, W. G., 67, 83–84

Weekly Register, 107

Whately, Richard, 32, 36–37, 39, 43, 45–46, 48, 72

White, Joseph Blanco, 36, 45

Wilberforce, Henry, 55, 66

Wiseman, Nicholas, Cardinal, Archbishop of Westminster, 60, 96, 98

Wootten, Frances, 104